Homes for a
Changing Climate
Passive Houses
in the U.S.

Katrin Klingenberg
Mike Kernagis
Mary James

Low Carbon Productions

Published in 2008 by
Low Carbon Productions
Larkspur, CA
www.lowcarbonproductions.com

Layout and design: Leanne Maxwell

This book is printed on 100% post-consumer
recycled paper that is acid free and has
Eco Logo and FSC certification.

Distributed by Chelsea Green Publishing

ISBN 9780615227405

Library of Congress Cataloging-in-Publication Data available

Printed in Canada

*This book represents the
views of the authors. Neither
PHIUS, e-co lab, Low Carbon
Productions, nor any person
acting on behalf of these
organizations is responsible
for any use that might be made
of the information contained
herein. The responsibility for
that information, including any
possible errors, remains with
the authors.*

Table of Contents

Foreword   i

Introduction   1

Chapter 1   Principles of Passive House Design   8

Chapter 2   The Smith House   19

Chapter 3   The Waldsee BioHaus   31

Chapter 4   The Fairview Houses   39

Chapter 5   The Cleveland Farm   49

Chapter 6   The Stanton House   59

Chapter 7   Toward a Passive House in a Hot-Humid Climate   69

Chapter 8   A Passive House Retrofit   79

Chapter 9   The Skyline House—a Passive House Challenge   86

Product Directory   93

Foreword

Prosperity and well-being in an industrial society depend on the availability of cheap energy. This was what almost all experts believed until 2003. Now, however, the consequences of accessing and using increasing amounts of energy are becoming apparent. Most nations are coming to depend more and more on imported oil, often from unstable regions; waste products from energy generation—whether from fossil fuels or nuclear power—are damaging the environment; and this damage is growing more severe as energy use increases. Burning any type of fossil fuel inevitably produces CO_2 as a byproduct; the nuclear industry generates highly radioactive wastes that must be safely stored for thousands of years. Uncertainty remains as to how the global community will be able to meet the ever-increasing demand for primary energy by a growing population with ever-increasing expectations, once cheap fossil fuels have been largely consumed.

If we choose not to ignore these problems, but rather to keep the facts clearly in mind, and take seriously the rights of future generations, it is clear that we must seek practical solutions immediately. If the solutions are not practical, they will not be adopted. Calls to curtail consumption or to change our lifestyle are not generally well received. A return to old-fashioned ideas will not help, either. Modern industrial society is a sensitive and sophisticated system, and amateurish attempts to change

Passivhaus Institut's founder and director Dr. Wolfgang Feist visits Katrin Klingenberg and tours the Fairview Houses in Urbana, Illinois.

it can cause great damage. Only well thought-out solutions and strategies can deliver the changes the world needs. Gradually implemented reforms are much preferable to a fast and forceful revolution.

One hopeful sign, and guiding precept, is the continual improvement of energy and material efficiency. Historically, all industrial development has been strongly influenced by efficiency improvements. The journey from the first steam engine to the modern gas power plant is a prime example of that progress. Every efficiency improvement implemented today reduces the amount of energy that will be needed tomorrow. If an efficiency measure is practical and economically feasible, then implementing that measure is equivalent to generating additional energy or "negawatts"—with the added benefit that these negawatts are truly sustainable, in that they have no harmful environmental impact, are permanent, and benefit everyone equally.

Efficiency as a guiding precept is ready to be implemented now. Indeed, efficiency solutions are within reach in all important industrial sectors, as the following examples show:

- In spring 2002, the chairman of Volkswagen's board of directors, Ferdinand Piëch, drove the prototype of a car that got 223.2 miles to the gallon to the annual board meeting in Hamburg. This represents an efficiency improvement of over 500% over the average efficiency of today's passenger cars.

- Recycled aluminum, PVC, and paper now supply the industrial manufacturing process with raw materials that cost only a fraction as much as new materials.

- Electronic paper, or e-paper, is a display technology that is now on the market. With microactuators that change color in response to a flexible array of transistors, e-paper is designed to mimic the appearance of ordinary ink on paper. It is completely flat and noiseless, and it uses a tiny fraction of the energy needed to power the display on a modern flat screen.

These are innovations that create lasting, effective solutions, using capital that is available today. But of all the industrial sectors, the building sector most convincingly demonstrates how effective comprehensive energy efficiency solutions can be:

- Research and industry have made glazing available that has a U-value of 0.5 to 0.7 W/m^{2}K (0.08–0.12 Btu/[h ft^2 F])—yielding 500% less thermal loss than typical double-pane windows.

- Small- to medium-sized businesses have developed innovative, highly insulated window frames that are now available in wood, plastic, or aluminum. These frames complement the advanced glazing, providing highly efficient window packages.

- Industrial manufacturers and builders have developed building components that sustain negligible heat loss, compared to traditional building components.

- Architects, engineers, and manufacturers have developed thermally broken structural connections that eliminate thermal bridges and air leaks, increasing occupant comfort and reducing heat loss.

- Architects, planners, and system providers have developed ventilation systems that function at a previously unimaginable level. With very little auxiliary energy input, these systems save over 90% of the energy that would otherwise be lost through the ventilation process, and still provide continuously fresh air throughout the building.

The integration of all of these developments into a functional whole, into a highly energy-efficient building concept, was mastered by the developers of the Passive House concept—a concept that reduces heating energy consumption not by a little, but by 90% or more. That sounds very technical, and it begs the question, Can one live in a box that is designed to save that much energy? Numerous progressive architects, courageous builders, and committed owners have answered Yes! Yes! Yes! The number of inhabited Passive Houses today approaches the tens of thousands. This number, and the variety of designs, prove that Passive Houses are not exotic research projects, but completely normal homes. Passive Houses are not full of complicated technology, but instead feature intuitive and simple devices—devices that any occupant can easily manage. And, as the U.S. case studies in this book clearly show, Passive House architecture is not monotonous or rigid, but creative and varied. And the windows can be opened!

The potential that flows from fostering new developments in efficiency is obvious. All that's needed is creativity to reach new perspectives—and courage, tolerance, and commitment. And for creativity to get translated into real payoffs, we need persistence, research and development, innovative strength, design ability, capital, continuing education, and craftsmanship, as well as work and services on all levels. Whom or what are we waiting for? Let's tackle it!

**Professor Wolfgang Feist,
University of Innsbruck, Austria
Founder, Passivhaus Insititut**

Widespread application of **Passive House** design principles and construction methods in the **United States** would **dramatically reduce** our country's **energy use**.

e-co lab

Introduction

As the consequences of climate change become increasingly obvious, it also becomes increasingly clear that all of us, including every business, must find ways to reduce our output of carbon emissions. This is particularly true for the building sector, which through both operations and construction-related activities contributes a large share of carbon emissions to the environment—from 40% to almost 50% of total U.S. emissions, depending on how the sector is defined. Knowing this, we must decide how best to square our need for energy to build and operate our houses with the needs of our environment—and of our pocketbook. The Passive House concept—which can slash space heating and cooling energy consumption of buildings by up to an amazing 90%—represents today's most rigorous energy standard and most compelling option. Thousands of homes have been built or remodeled to meet the Passive House standard in Europe. Widespread application of Passive House design principles and construction methods here in the United States would dramatically reduce our country's energy use.

Conceived in North America

The Passive House evolved from the superinsulated buildings of the 1970s, many of which were built in North America. The Small Homes Council of the University of Illinois developed the Lo-Cal house in the late '70s, and Wayne Schick, a member of the architectural faculty, is credited with coining the term "superinsulation." The Arkansas Project, the Canadian National Research Council, and Minnesota's Housing Finance Agency also supported the construction of very low-energy prototypes. In 1981, William Shurcliff, a Harvard physicist, published *Superinsulated and Double-Envelope Houses*, a book that to this day provides a wealth of detail on the topic. Many of these early prototypes are still comfortable, energy-efficient homes with very good indoor air quality (IAQ).

However, it was in Europe that the first true Passive Houses were built. The movement toward the construction of these houses received a big push from the passage of a rigorous energy standard for new buildings in Sweden in 1988. In response, Swedish professor Bo Adamson and German physicist Wolfgang Feist designed a building that could meet and even exceed this standard—the Passive House. The first prototype, a four-unit row house structure, was built in 1990 in Darmstadt, Germany. Then as now, the primary components of a Passive House were thick insulation, few or no thermal bridges, an airtight envelope, insulated glazing, and balanced energy recovery ventilation.

The Passive House, or Passivhaus in German, was so called because, in the relatively cold, heating-dominated Central European climate, it required so little energy to heat that a conventional heating system could be eliminated and replaced by one 1,000-watt electric-resistance heater. Such homes could be kept warm passively, that is, by using existing internal heat sources—people, lights, and appliances; solar energy admitted by the windows; and a fresh-air supply that would be warmed by, for example, an earth tube, which is a passive geothermal heating-and-cooling system. Monitoring of the first and other early prototypes found the maximum heat load in the German winter to be less than 10 watts per square meter (W/m^2), or 0.9 watts per square foot (W/ft^2), of floor area. Under these circumstances, the heat load could be comfortably supplied using fresh-air ventilation—eliminating the need for a separate means of heat distribution—or any active-solar contribution.

Supported by research grants from the German state of Hesse, Dr. Feist created detailed computerized simulations modeling the energy behaviors of wall and window assemblies and other construction elements. Then he systematically varied these elements to arrive at the best possible construction packages, based on energy efficiency, installation expense, and sustainability. In 1995, American energy visionary Amory Lovins visited the Passive House at Darmstadt. Lovins' own Rocky Mountain Institute headquarters building, which was completed in 1984, is a prime example of superinsulated construction. He was deeply impressed by the building's low energy use, and encouraged Dr. Feist to view this project as a practical means of meeting housing and energy needs. All that was needed was to redesign some details to reduce construction costs.

In 1996, Dr. Feist founded the Passivhaus Institut (PHI) in Darmstadt. Until very recently, he lived in the original prototype in Darmstadt and biked to the PHI every day. The PHI has flourished under his leadership, designing, testing, calculating, certifying, and analyzing data on Passive Houses and their components. The Passive House Planning Package (PHPP) is the Institut's energy-modeling program. The methodology used in this program is profoundly thorough, and it has been used to design thousands of projects across Europe.

The Passive House standard is the lowest energy standard in Europe. It requires that

Katrin Klingenberg (pictured above) and Passive House builder Mike Kernagis cofounded the Passive House Institute United States (PHIUS) to disseminate information about, and promote the construction of, Passive Houses in this country.

a building use no more than 15 kilowatt-hours per square meter (kWh/m^2) per year in heating energy, and no more than 15 kWh/m^2 in cooling energy, which is equivalent to 1.35 kWh/ft^2 or 4.8 thousand British thermal units per square foot ($kBtu/ft^2$), for each use annually. It further requires that the building's total primary energy consumption—that is, source energy used for space conditioning, hot water, and electricity—not exceed 120 kWh/m^2 (10.8 kWh/ft^2 or 38 $kBtu/ft^2$) per year. (Source energy is the amount of energy that must be generated at a power plant to deliver a useful unit of energy to a house. Generally there are such large efficiency losses during production and delivery of electricity that roughly 3 units of source energy must be generated for each 1 unit of electricity that is used on site.)

Passive Houses—and the techniques and products developed for them—were further popularized in Europe through the European Union–sponsored Cost Efficient Passive Houses as European Standards (CEPHEUS) project, which validated that the Passive House concept worked in five European countries over the winter of 2000–2001. Today, thousands of Passive Houses have been built across Europe, as interest in the benefits that they provide has skyrocketed. Many provinces and cities there are now mandating that all new construction built with public monies be built to the Passive House standard. As of this writing, there was an action plan before the parliament of the European Union (EU) urging the adoption of the standard across the EU.

Back in the U.S.A.

In the spring of 2002, German-born architect Katrin Klingenberg traveled from the United States, where she currently lives, to Germany to tour Passive Houses with Manfred Brausem, a leading builder and Passive House pioneer there. An ardent advocate of sustainable architecture, Klingenberg was powerfully affected by what she saw. She returned to the United States and began designing her own Passive House, the Smith House, which broke ground that October in Urbana, Illinois. In 2003, Klingenberg attended the Seventh International Passive House Conference, in Hamburg, where she met Dr. Feist. She returned to finish the Smith House, which became the first Passive House in North America, according to Dr. Feist. Monitoring devices installed after its completion at the Smith House, which has no solar thermal or PV system, show some pleasing numbers. The house uses only 11 kWh/m^2 (1 kWh/ft^2 or 3.5 $kBtu/ft^2$) per year in heating energy.

The highest monthly energy use ever for space and water heating, appliances, and lighting—in short, for all purposes—was 599 kWh. With an average electrical base load of 265 kWh, the highest monthly energy use for space heating has been 334 kWh. (For more about this house, see chapter 2, "The Smith House.")

Knowing that the best way to promote Passive Houses in the United States was to get them built and monitored, Klingenberg started the Ecological Construction Laboratory (e-co lab), a nonprofit community housing development organization, in 2004. E-co lab's mission is to design, build, sell, and monitor Passive Houses for low-income home buyers. E-co lab's first project, the Fairview House, was constructed in 2006 and sold to a woman who had been displaced from New Orleans by Hurricane Katrina. It was built to perform in the rigorous climate of Illinois, with 14-inch walls of high-density blown-in fiberglass and an airtightness measuring 0.24 air changes per hour (ACH) at 50 pascals (Pa) of pressure. (More details on this house can be found in chapter 4, "The Fairview Houses.")

In 2005, Klingenberg met Stephan Tanner, a Swiss-born architect who was working on another American Passive House, the BioHaus in Bemidji, Minnesota—an even more challenging climate. Designed as a learning facility for the German-language Concordia Village, the BioHaus succeeded in meeting the Passive House standard and was certified by the PHI in 2006. (More information on this house can be found in chapter 3, "The Waldsee BioHaus.") In October 2006, Klingenberg and Tanner teamed up to organize the first North American Passive House conference at the BioHaus. It was attended by a number of Midwestern building science professionals—architects, engineers, builders, and energy researchers and consultants—but there were also professionals from New England and the Southwest. Discussions about housing energy needs generally and the Passive House concept specifically ensued, and presenters went on to introduce the first Passive Houses built in the States: the Smith House, the BioHaus, and the first Fairview House. Interest was piqued; new projects were started.

Climate-Changing Opportunity

Klingenberg has steadily promoted Passive Houses at symposia, workshops, and conferences from coast to coast. In April 2007, Klingenberg and Passive House builder Mike Kernagis cofounded the Passive House Institute United States (PHIUS) to disseminate information about, and promote the construction of, Passive Houses in this country. Currently Passive House projects are under way in climates as varied as Martha's Vineyard, Massachusetts; Duluth, Minnesota; and Santa Fe and Taos, New Mexico. Although most Passive House construction to date consists of new buildings, one retrofit project is architect Nabih Tahan's treatment of his own home in Berkeley, California. Tahan undertook retrofitting to Passive House standards because he had seen the value of this type of construction at first hand, having lived and worked for many years in Austria. (This house is further described in chapter 8, "A Passive House Retrofit.")

In addition to consulting on Passive House projects around the country, Klingenberg is currently designing prefabricated components that reduce the cost of building Passive Houses, components she has employed on the second Fairview House and a newer project, the Stanton House. "It has to be affordable," says Klingenberg. "As Amory Lovins says, 'We need to tunnel through the cost barrier.' There is a lot of work that needs to be done, on a lot of levels, to make the necessary reductions in greenhouse gas emissions possible. But there's a lot of opportunity there, too. Our emphasis is energy efficiency. There's so much to be conserved, and we'd like to see that valued appropriately. Let's get as much as we reasonably can out of efficient design, and then apply active-solar elements. This way we are in a position to have plus-energy homes, while running the most climate-neutral buildings we can."

In November 2007, e-co lab and PHIUS held the second North American Passive House conference and tour in Urbana, Illinois. Among the presenters were longtime

Prefabricated wall panels can cut the costs and the time needed to build a Passive House, without sacrificing high-quality building practices.

trailblazers Harold Orr, Bill Rose, and Marc Rosenbaum, and German Passive House builder Manfred Brausem. They were joined by presenters of projects under way in California, New Mexico, Minnesota, Illinois, and Massachusetts. Developers of Passive House communities in Colorado and Michigan presented as well. Attendance increased dramatically over attendance in 2006, with about 100 participants from 21 different states. As of this writing, PHIUS has scheduled the third conference and tour, taking place in November 2008 in Duluth, Minnesota, where there is a strong and growing regional interest. In May 2008, PHIUS introduced a training program for Passive House consultants. Building industry professionals are taught the principles of Passive House design; use of the PHPP, materials, and mechanical systems; and quality assurance. As with other PHIUS initiatives, response has been strong, and there are now about 25 certified Passive House consultants nationwide.

This book was written to disseminate information about Passive House design and construction methods and to promote an approach to home building that best meets today's energy and environmental needs. The Passive House concept is a timely and powerful solution that is only now gaining traction in the United States. Many Passive House projects in this country are so new that empirical data on their energy performance are limited, but extensive data on the energy performance of Passive Houses in Europe are available through the CEPHEUS project at www.passivehouse.com/ 07_eng/news/CEPHEUS_final_long.pdf.

A sense of urgency about the need to reduce the housing sector's carbon emissions led us to bring out what we conceive of as an inaugural volume.

Outstanding Passive House projects are now in design and under construction all over the United States. Stylish single-family homes are being built in Illinois, Minnesota, and Indiana; in Maine, Massachusetts, and New York; in California, Arizona, Colorado, and New Mexico; and in Oregon and Washington. Some of these homes experiment with construction materials, heat sources, or solar-thermal storage; others make use of natural ventilation or other innovative cooling methods. Some will generate more energy than they use. There are also multifamily projects slated for Illinois, Michigan, Ohio, Massachusetts, and Colorado; some of these will be reserved for low- and fixed-income tenants. We are thrilled to promote the creation of truly high-performance buildings here in North America in every way that we can.

For more information:

The **Passive House Institute United States (PHIUS)** is an energy calculating, consulting, and research firm working to further the implementation of Passive House standards nationwide. For information about the institute, go to **www.passivehouse.us.**

For more about the **e-co lab**, go to **www.e-colab.org**.

Chapter 1

Principles of Passive House Design

The Passive House concept is a comprehensive approach to cost-effective, high-quality, healthy, and sustainable construction. It seeks to achieve two goals: minimizing energy losses and maximizing passive energy gains. Simple enough. But achieving these goals has led to extraordinary results—a Passive House uses up to 90% less energy for space heating and cooling than a conventionally constructed house. The Passive House standard is the world's most rigorous standard for energy-efficient construction.

To attain such outstanding energy savings, Passive House designers and builders work together to systematically implement the following seven principles:

- Superinsulate.
- Eliminate thermal bridges.
- Make it airtight.
- Specify energy or heat recovery ventilation.
- Specify high-performance windows and doors.
- Optimize passive-solar and internal heat gains.
- Model energy gains and losses using the PHPP.

The **Passive House** standard is the world's **most rigorous standard** for **energy-efficient** construction.

Superinsulate

The insulation applied to a house works in much the same way as the insulation on a thermos bottle. In both cases, the insulating outer shell or envelope blocks or slows heat transmission and maintains the contents at a relatively constant temperature. Warm contents stay warm, cool contents stay cool, even when the temperature on the outside hits one extreme or the other. In a Passive House, the entire envelope of the building—walls, roof, and floor or basement—is well insulated. How well insulated? That depends, of course, on the climate. To achieve the Passive

House standard, Nabih Tahan's house in Berkeley, California, required only 6 inches of blown-in cellulose insulation, while the Skyline House, in the far harsher climate of Duluth, Minnesota, needed 16 inches—almost 3 times as much. Often the first feature of a Passive House to catch a visitor's attention is the unusual thickness of the walls. This thickness is needed to accommodate the required level of insulation.

Even with this insulation requirement, Passive House designers have a wide range of choices for the materials used to create superinsulated building envelopes. Wall assemblies can be built using conventional lumber or masonry construction, double-stud construction, structural insulated panels (SIPs), insulated concrete forms (ICFs), truss joist I-beams (TJIs), steel, or strawbale construction. Similarly, designers can choose from a number of different types of insulation. These include cellulose, high-density blown-in fiberglass, polystyrene, spray foam, and—again—strawbale. Although spray foams have a high R-value and are easy to apply, many builders prefer not to use them, because they are petroleum-based products, and because the foaming agents can deplete the ozone layer and contribute to global warming. Manufacturers are seeking to develop spray foams that do not have these disadvantages. Vacuum insulated panels (VIPs) are a relatively new, and as yet pricey, option with an exceptionally high R-value per inch. Using VIPs allows designers and builders to greatly decrease the thickness of the walls in homes where that is a consideration. Still higher-tech insulations are in development.

No matter which type of insulation gets chosen, Passive House builders need to make sure that the product is installed correctly. The application and performance of insulation can be directly measured using thermographic imaging. All objects emit infrared (IR) radiation, and the amount of radiation emitted increases with the temperature of the object. Variations in IR radiation, and therefore in temperature, can be observed using a thermographic, or IR, camera—a useful tool for testing buildings. Since these cameras can readily detect heat loss, they can usually identify areas where insulation is insufficient, incomplete, damaged, or settled. Technicians who read thermal images of properly constructed Passive Houses have jokingly called them boring, as they often reveal little substantive heat loss.

Eliminate Thermal Bridges

Heat will flow out of a building on the easiest available path, the path of least resistance. It will pass very quickly through an element that has a higher thermal conductivity than the surrounding material, forming what is known as a thermal bridge. Thermal bridges can significantly increase heat loss, which can create areas in or on the walls that are cooler than their surroundings. In the worst-case scenario, this can cause moisture problems, when warm, moist air condenses on a cooler surface.

Thermal bridges can occur at edges, corners, connections, and penetrations. A bridge can be as simple as a single lintel that has a higher thermal conductivity than the surrounding wall or several steel wall ties that pass through an envelope. A balcony slab that is not insulated from, and thus thermally isolated from, an interior concrete floor can be a potent thermal bridge. An effective thermal isolation is called a thermal break. Without a thermal break, the balcony will act as a very large cooling fin—in the wintertime!

In a Passive House, there are few or no thermal bridges. When the thermal bridge coefficient, which is an indicator of the extra heat loss caused by a thermal bridge, is less than .01 watts per meter per Kelvin (W/mK), the detail or wall assembly is said to be thermal bridge free. Additional heat loss through this detail is negligible, and interior temperatures are sufficiently stabilized to eliminate moisture problems. It is critical for the Passive House designer and builder to plan to reduce or eliminate thermal bridges by limiting penetrations, and by using heat transfer–resistant materials. Thermographic imaging can be used to determine how effective the efforts to eliminate thermal bridges have been.

Make It Airtight

Airtight construction helps the performance of a building by reducing or eliminating drafts —whether hot or cold—thereby reducing the need for space conditioning. Airtightness also helps to prevent warm, moist air penetrating the structure, condensing inside the wall, and causing structural damage.

Airtight construction is achieved by wrapping an intact, continuous layer of airtight materials around the entire building envelope. Special care must be taken to ensure the continuity of this layer around windows, doors, penetrations, and all joints between the roof, walls, and floors. Insulation materials are generally not airtight; the materials used to create an intact airtight layer include various membranes, tapes, plasters, glues, shields, and gaskets. These materials are becoming increasingly durable, adherent, easy to apply, and environmentally sound, which in turn is making it easier for a builder to meet the stringent airtightness requirement of the Passive House standard.

The airtightness of a house provides a measurable dimension of the quality of construction. Testing airtightness requires the use of a blower door, which is essentially a large specialized fan. The blower door can be used to either depressurize or pressurize a house to a designated pressure. With the fan set to maintain this designated pressure, a technician can assess how much air is infiltrating the building through all its gaps and cracks. Specific leaks can be detected during the test either by hand, by employing tracer smoke, or by looking at thermographic images. It is best to conduct the blower door test at a point in construction when the airtight layer can still be easily accessed and any leaks can be readily addressed. Passive Houses are extremely tight. At a standard test pressure of 50 Pa, a Passive House must allow no more than 0.6 ACH in order to achieve certification. Passive Houses built from timber, masonry, prefabricated elements, and steel framing members have all met this standard.

Airtightness does not mean that you can't open the windows! Passive Houses have fully operable windows, and most are designed to take full advantage of natural ventilation to help maintain comfortable temperatures in the spring, fall, and even summer, depending on the local climate.

Specify Energy and Heat Recovery Ventilation

Perhaps the most common misperception regarding Passive Houses concerns airflow. "A house needs to breathe," builders might say disapprovingly, when first presented with the idea of building very tight homes. Well, a Passive House does breathe—exceptionally well. However, rather than breathing unknown volumes of

Contractors get ready to apply fiber cement siding planks to Fairview I, a Passive House built for low-income, first-time home buyers. The furring strips create a cavity behind the siding that acts as a rain screen and allows for convective cooling in the summer.

air through uncontrolled leaks, Passive Houses breathe controlled volumes of air by mechanical ventilation. Mechanical ventilation circulates measured amounts of fresh air through the house and exhausts known quantities of stale air from the house. This makes for excellent IAQ. The health and comfort of the occupants come first for the Passive House designer, and excellent IAQ is indispensable for occupant health.

A Passive House is ventilated using a balanced mechanical ventilation system. Needless to say, this ventilation system must be extremely energy efficient. To that end, Passive House designers specify energy recovery ventilators (ERVs) or heat recovery ventilators (HRVs) in cold, dry climates. These machines incorporate an air-to-air energy recovery system, which conserves most of the energy in the exhaust air and transfers it to the incoming fresh air. This significantly reduces the energy needed to heat that incoming air. State-of-the-art ventilation systems have heat recovery rates of 75% to 95%.

The ventilation system generally exhausts air from the rooms that produce moisture and odors, such as the kitchen and bathrooms. Humidistats installed in these rooms monitor when moisture levels are elevated, initiating an increase in the ventilation flow rate. The exhaust air gets drawn through the ventilator on its way out of the building. There it passes through a heat exchanger that transfers the reusable heat energy to the incoming fresh air. It is important to note that the exhaust air is not mixed with the incoming air; only its heat is transferred. Indeed, while return air is circulated back to the furnace in a forced-air system, no air is recirculated with a mechanical ventilation system.

When operating, the ventilator provides a constant supply of fresh air. At the same time, it removes excess moisture, odors, and any noxious gases. The incoming air is filtered and balanced. It is distributed at a generally low flow rate through small, unobtrusive, but highly effective, diffusers. The system is generally very quiet and draft free. The PHPP recommends an ACH of 0.3 to 0.4 times the volume of the building, and a guideline ACH of 30 cubic meters (m^3) per person.

The main difference between an HRV and an ERV is that the HRV conserves heat and cooling energy, while the ERV does this and transfers humidity as well. In summer, an ERV helps keep the humidity outside; in winter, it helps prevent indoor air from becoming too dry. For in-between seasons, when no conditioning is needed, a bypass can be installed for either system to avoid heating the incoming air. Alternatively, the ventilation system can be turned off altogether, and windows can be thrown open to bring in fresh air.

Either system's efficiency can be increased by prewarming or precooling the incoming air. This is done by passing the incoming air through earth tubes. Since the ground maintains a more consistent temperature throughout the year than the outdoors, passing the air through tubes buried in the earth either preheats or precools the air, depending on the season. Preheating and precooling can also be accomplished indirectly, by circulating water in an underground pipe and using it to heat or cool the air with a water-to-air heat exchanger.

Specify High-Performance Windows and Doors

In modeling the energy of a building, the designers of Passive Houses choose windows and doors based largely on their insulating value. It used to be hard to find doors and windows that did not conduct heat, and the few that existed were very expensive. However, that is no longer the case. There have been extraordinary advances in window quality over the past 30 years, and thermal losses from windows have dropped dramatically. Many brands of windows and doors are now being made tighter, reducing losses through infiltration and exfiltration. Doors have been provided with appropriate thermal breaks and double gaskets. Overall, high-performance windows and doors are proving to be cost-effective in Passive House applications.

One development that has significantly affected the heat conductivity of windows is the introduction of low-emissivity (low-e) coatings. These are microscopically thin, transparent layers of metal or metallic oxide deposited on the surface of the glass. The coated side of the glass faces into the gap between the two panes of a double-glazed window. The gap is filled with low-conductivity argon or krypton gas rather than air,

greatly reducing the window's radiant heat transfer. Different low-e coatings have been designed to allow for high, moderate, or low solar gain. This provides a range of options for houses in all climates, from heating dominated to cooling dominated. Today, builders can choose to install triple-pane, low-e-coated, argon-filled windows with special low-conductivity spacers and insulated, thermally broken frames. These windows eliminate any perceptible cold radiation or convective cold airflow, even in periods of heavy frost.

Optimize Passive-Solar and Internal Heat Gains

Not only must designers of Passive Houses minimize energy loss, they must also carefully manage energy gains. The first step in designing a Passive House is to consider how the orientation of the building—and its various parts—will affect its energy losses and gains. There are many issues to be considered. Where should the glazing be to allow for maximum sunlight when sunlight is wanted, and minimal heat gain when heat gain is unwanted? The more direct natural lighting there is, the less energy will be needed to provide light. Designers can enhance occupants' enjoyment of available sunlight by orienting bedrooms and living rooms to the south, and putting utility rooms and closets, where sunlight is not needed, to the north.

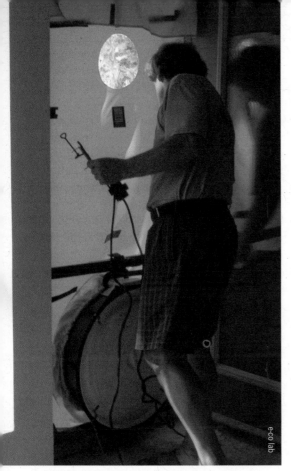

James Anderson of the University of Illinois' Building Research Council performs a blower door test to measure the airtightness of a Passive House.

e-co lab

However, it is not always possible to site a house in this ideal way. There may be buildings, trees, or landforms that cast shadows during short winter days, blocking out much of the low sunlight. Or the designer may need to accommodate the homeowner's demand for a certain view—a view that would not be available in an ideal orientation.

Windows are designed, oriented, and installed to take advantage of the outstanding passive-solar energy that can be gained through them. But the goal is not simply to allow for as much solar gain as possible. Some early superinsulated buildings suffered from overheating, because not enough consideration was given to the amount of solar gain that the house would experience. A good design should balance solar gain within the home's overall conditioning needs—and within the glazing budget. Even very efficient windows can lose more heat over a year than they gain, depending on their location, and large windows are expensive.

In the Northern Hemisphere, in climates dominated by heating loads, windows on the north allow for no direct solar heat gain, while those on the south allow for a great deal of it. In summertime, and in primarily cooling climates, it is very important to prevent excess solar heat gain. This can be done by shading the windows. Roof eaves of the proper length can effectively shade south-facing windows when the sun is higher in the summer, and still allow for maximum solar heat gain in the winter, when the sun is lower and the days are colder. Deciduous trees or vines on a trellis can also block out sunlight in the summer and admit it in the winter.

In climates that have a significant cooling load, the designer should consider limiting unshaded east- and west-facing windows, and specifying only windows that have low-solar-gain, low-e coatings. During the morning and late afternoon, low-angled sunlight can generate a great deal of heat in such windows.

Another, perhaps less obvious, source of heat gain is internal. Given the exceptionally low levels of heat loss in a Passive House, heat from internal sources can make quite a difference. Household appliances, electronic equipment, artificial lighting, candles, people—all can have a significant effect on the heat gain in a Passive House. While designers may not choose the appliances that are installed in a house, they often select the lighting sources, and they must take into account the heat gain from those sources when they calculate overall internal heat gain.

Use the PHPP for Energy Modeling

There are many elements of Passive House design that need to be integrated with one another. They include wall thickness, R- or U-values, thermal bridges, airtightness, ventilation sizing, windows, solar orientation, climate, and energy gains and losses. The PHPP is a powerful and accurate energy-modeling tool that helps a designer to integrate each of these elements into the design, so that the final design will meet the Passive House standard.

The PHPP starts with the whole building as one zone of energy calculation. The designer inputs all of the basic characteristics of the house—orientation, size, location of windows, insulation levels, and so on. The PHPP can even be used to model such advanced features as solar water heating for combined space and water heating, or the contributions of natural ventilation to nighttime cooling. The PHPP then computes the energy balance of the design. If needed, the designer can change one or more elements—the size or location of a window, for example—within the PHPP and model the effect of those changes on the overall energy balance. Experienced Passive House designers often work with their drawing programs and their PHPP both open. The Passive House standard is met when

- *the space heating and cooling requirements of the design are each less than or equal to 15 kWh per square meter per year (kWh/m²a) (4.8 kBtu/ft²/yr);*

- *the primary (source) energy use of the design is less than or equal to 120 kWh/m²a (38.1 kBtu/ft²/yr); and*

- *the airtightness of the building is verified to be at or below 0.6 ACH @50Pa.*

A Word on Cooling and Dehumidification

The Passive House concept was developed primarily in Central Europe, which has a relatively mild, primarily heating-oriented climate. Implementation of designs that meet the Passive House standard is more challenging in extremely cold, hot, or humid climates. Nevertheless, many Passive Houses have already been built in very cold climates, and Passive Houses are now starting to be built in hotter climates.

In cooling load (as in heating load) situations, the space conditioning load must be minimized. This takes careful planning. As we explained earlier, the high levels of insulation in a Passive House help to keep indoor temperatures cool. In addition to the standard measures for preventing excess solar gain, convective venting behind siding and roofing and night cooling will often suffice to maintain indoor comfort. In humid climates, an additional cooling load may stem from the need to remove latent moisture from the air. A very small and efficient air-to-air heat pump—also known as a mini-split—can remove this moisture and provide adequate cooling.

This prefabricated panel is framed with 12-inch wooden I-joists set upright at 24 inches on center, and sheathed with structural fiberboard on the exterior and oriented strand board on the interior. It is filled with a high-density fiberglass insulation.

Economic Sustainability

Passive House design focuses on balancing energy gains and losses to attain a level of energy efficiency that is far beyond the norm. But the norm is changing, and many people now recognize that energy efficiency is profoundly important, both economically and environmentally. It has been called a low-hanging fruit, an innovation that can, and should, be readily attained.

This focus on energy efficiency makes Passive Houses more expensive to build. Construction costs generally run 10% to 15% higher than construction costs for a conventional house. The additional up-front costs of more insulation, better windows and doors, and more labor for higher-quality installations are partially offset by the lower cost of the heating-and-cooling systems. Because Passive Houses have such small heating-and-cooling requirements, conventional heating-and-cooling systems can be replaced with miniaturized components and efficient mechanical ventilation. This is one example of how the integrated planning required to build a Passive House helps builders to "tunnel through the cost barrier," in the words of Amory Lovins. The additional construction cost is readily recuperated in savings on the homeowner's energy bill. These savings will continue throughout the life of the house. And—perhaps most important in the long run—the Passive House will generate a carbon footprint that is a fraction of the size of that of a conventional house. On-site renewable-energy resources can be added to create a true zero-energy, or even plus-energy, house—one that produces more power than it consumes.

In the past, most homes were built with scant attention paid to their long-term energy consumption. This approach needs to change. We need to use our limited natural resources wisely, and we need to build our homes with quality and durability in mind. The costs of energy consumption are high, and they are going higher. The savings to be realized over the life of a Passive House are remarkable, both economically and environmentally.

For more information:

To learn more about the **Passivhaus Institut**, visit **www.passivehouse.com**

For information from the Passivhaus Institut that has been translated into English, go to **www.passivhaustagung.de/Passive_House_E/ PassiveHouse_directory.html**

For more information on Passive Houses in Europe, visit **www.passive-on.org.**

Chapter 2
The Smith House

Completed in 2003, the Smith House in Urbana, Illinois, was the first house built in the United States to the Passive House standard.

The Smith House is the first of three Passive Houses built in Urbana, Illinois, to date. Constructed in 2002–2003, it was the first house built in the United States using the specific practices, technologies, and energy-modeling tools developed by the PHI to achieve the Passive House standard. Dr. Feist modeled the Smith House's energy losses and gains and used it as the first English-language sample project to be entered into the newly translated PHPP 2004. The Smith House is listed among other Passive Houses in the PHI database, although Klingenberg, the designer and owner, has never sought to have it officially certified. Passive House certification is a voluntary process of having energy calculations and details checked by an independent institution to determine if the project has been planned and built in accordance with the standard requirements. A blower-door test is required to prove that airtightness goals have been met. The certifying agency in Europe is the PHI. PHIUS became the certifying agency in the U.S. in 2008.

By coincidence, serendipity, or perhaps fate, the Smith House came into being in a place that has a remarkable history when it comes to developing superinsulated homes. The Small Homes Council of the University of Illinois helped develop prototypes of very low-energy homes, as we explained in the introduction. Many of the pioneers of superinsulation are still teaching at the University of Illinois Urbana-Champaign and are well-known experts in the field of high-performance building. With this history, Urbana has more than its share of superinsulated houses, and all that are still in use are maintaining their value in a marketplace that is increasingly concerned with energy use, IAQ, and operation costs.

In 2000, Klingenberg and her husband, Nic Smith, were both working for a very successful architecture firm in Chicago, famous for its high-end commercial and urban architecture. Many of the firm's projects made use of innovative energy efficiency and natural-ventilation strategies, such as double-glazed walls for high-rises. However, the measured results of those strategies were rather disappointing. As it turned out, they reduced overall building energy consumption by only about 30%.

Then, in 2000, the United States withdrew from the Kyoto Protocol.

This action prompted Klingenberg to search even harder for a way to leapfrog from conventional architecture to a carbon-neutral and economically feasible approach to building, without getting bogged down in incrementalism. It inspired her search for a path that would lead away from dependence on an oil-based economy and toward the creation of a global economy based on sustainable energy and equity.

This was also the year when Klingenberg set foot in her first-ever Passive House, at the World Expo in Hannover. In preparation for the Expo, the city of Hannover had adopted the Hannover Principles, which specified that all design and construction related to the fair would represent sustainable development. The house was part of the Kronsberg development, the first carbon-neutral development in Hannover that had been commissioned for the Expo by Hannover's city council. This was a life-changing moment for Klingenberg. There it was—the answer to the question she had been posing for herself: How much energy can you afford to use in your home if your goal is to mitigate climate change and to help create a global economy based on sustainable energy?

In 1992, climate scientists at the United Nations Earth Summit in Rio de Janeiro had answered that question theoretically. They concluded that to stabilize the earth's atmosphere and prevent global warming, energy use and greenhouse gas emissions must be cut by a factor of 10. The building scientists and architects who developed the Passive House concept had taken this recommendation to heart. They studied high-performance homes around the world—including those in the United States—closely examining passive-solar and superinsulation techniques, and arrived at an answer that had been unthinkable until then. Yes, we can build homes that use 90% less energy—for a price people can afford—by employing efficiency techniques. We don't need to rely on costly active-solar technologies.

As soon as they saw the Passive House in Hannover, Klingenberg and Smith decided to build a prototype in the United States. They chose to build in Urbana, where Smith had grown up, not knowing that superinsulated homes already had a history in that city. Klingenberg and Smith designed the house together, but Smith died before it was completed. The house was named after him in his memory.

Ecological Decisions

The Smith House was designed with a number of goals in mind. First, its operational energy use must be reduced by a factor of 10. Second, the design must follow cradle-to-cradle principles as closely as possible. That is, all the components of the house must be high in recycled content, and they must be

Yes, we can build homes that use **90% less energy**—for a price people can **afford**—by employing **efficiency techniques.**

reusable or recyclable at the end of the home's useful life. Third, building materials must be chosen with their environmental impact in mind. This meant purchasing locally and sustainably harvested wood products and locally manufactured building products whenever possible. Finally, Klingenberg wanted to be sure that the house would fit well within her goal of minimizing her personal environmental impact. To reduce travel-related emissions, Klingenberg chose a site that was close to the city. There is even a local bus stop right in front of the house.

Trellises and outdoor rooms, like the small porch on the east side of the house and the space under and above the deck, form transition spaces to the plant life around the house. The "lawn" to the east of the house is planted in prairie grass; it will eventually spread, reducing the overall area that needs mowing. Plantings and gardens follow permaculture principles. Chickens are allowed in Urbana, and Klingenberg sees a few in her future, as soon as everybody starts building Passive Houses and her work is done. "I can retire, and with the time on my hands I will build a chicken coop and add a couple of chickens to my life," she says. "At that point, I will almost be able to provide everything I need to live on from my half-acre land. I won't need very much money, because my house is almost self-sufficient. If it's not quite warm enough in the winter, I will light a few candles, and my comfort level will be greater than it has been in all the other spaces that I have lived in before."

Building a new home was a financially challenging project for two young professionals who were having to raise all of the funds needed to cover construction costs by themselves. The budget was tight enough that it did not allow for the immediate installation of a photovoltaic (PV) or a rainwater catchment system—both features that Klingenberg wants, and that would have made the home more self-sufficient. But preparations were made for adding these features in the future. One set of conduits will make it possible to use rainwater to flush the toilets, while another set will bring rainwater from a cistern to the washing machine. Conduits into the mechanical room, additional electric wiring, and grid shutoffs will make it easier to install PV panels. Even the shape of the roof and the roofing material were chosen with an eye to facilitating the installation of these features.

The Floor Plan

The Smith House is a two-bedroom single-family residence with a finished floor area of 1,200 square feet, including a double-story space above the living room. The living room, kitchen, mechanical room, and bathroom are located on the first floor. The living room faces a generously glazed south wall, with a door that opens to a patio that is finished with 2-foot by 2-foot concrete tiles. A trellis of grapevines provides excellent shading for the first floor in the summer; an overhang shades the windows on the second floor. In the fall, the grapevine loses its leaves just in time to admit the sunlight needed to warm the house.

The ceiling of the living room extends to the roof, with a gallery on the second floor. The second floor resembles a loft; one bedroom is closed off from the gallery, but the other is open to the gallery along its entire width. The vaulted ceiling of this room goes all the way up to the north edge of the roof. This room is defined only by a painting, 8 feet high by 9 feet wide, which serves as a sliding door across the full width of the room, separating it from the gallery and the second bedroom. A 12-foot by 8-foot cedar deck on the west side of the building opens off the gallery. It is a favorite spot for watching the sunset. In the fall, Klingenberg can stand on this deck and pick pears from a 100-year-old pear tree in the garden.

The Best Shape, the Best Orientation

The Smith House is known to the locals as the contemporary one for its simple, compact shape.

Truss joist I-beams and laminated veneer lumber form the structural skeleton of the Smith House.

This shape conserves energy, because it results in the smallest possible surface-to-volume ratio, and the smaller this ratio, the less heat is lost by transmission through the roof and walls.

The Smith House's simple shed roof slopes toward the south, which is contrary to traditional passive-solar design. This orientation was chosen for several reasons. First, Klingenberg and Smith wanted a loft space that would open to the south. Second, they wanted the roof to face south as well to provide the maximum solar exposure for a planned PV system. The result was a one-and-a-half-story glass wall on the south, and a loft space above the living room whose ceiling height starts on the south end at 6 feet and rises gradually to 8½ feet on the north end.

Urbana is an area that receives a fair amount of sunshine over the course of a year, which bodes well for the productivity of a PV system. But what's good for a PV system—ample sunshine, even in winter—can create problems for the rest of the house, as early passive-solar homeowners found out. Large amounts of south-facing glazing can admit enough solar gain to warm or even overheat a house in winter during the daytime but, when the sun sets, those large windows can lose a fair amount of heat, causing uncomfortable daily temperature swings. Choosing to slope the roof toward the south also helped Klingenberg to avoid this problem, as this reduced the size of the south-facing façade, and therefore the size of the south-facing glazing area, while maintaining pleasing window-to-wall proportions.

For optimal solar heat gain in winter, a house in Urbana should be oriented due south (although up to 30° out of true south is acceptable for a Passive House), and all windows on the south façade should have a high solar heat gain coefficient (SHGC). Oriented toward true south, the Smith House has both of these advantages.

Overhangs and a trellis provide exterior shading, as we explained above. This prevents unwanted solar gain from increasing the cooling load in the summer.

Windows facing east and west are generally harder to shade in the summer than windows facing north and south, because they are exposed to many hours of low-angled sun. Overhangs cannot block sunlight coming in at a low angle; only vertical exterior shading will do so. To minimize unwanted solar gain and overheating in the summer, the windows on the north, east, and west sides of the Smith House are kept to a minimum, and those windows have a low SHGC.

All of the windows in the Smith House are operable. This makes it possible to take full advantage of the wind, whichever direction it is coming from, to maximize natural ventilation. Windows placed high up on the north side of the house give warmer air an easy exit, when the mechanical ventilation is turned off, allowing natural ventilation to take over.

The Best Envelope for Central Illinois

Climate and location determine the appropriate level of insulation for a Passive House. One of the first factors to consider is an area's winter design temperature, which is the lowest temperature that an area generally experiences in winter. Urbana has a winter design temperature of −3°F. This is considerably lower than the winter design temperature of Berlin at 7°F and Paris at 22°F, for example—climates for which many Passive Homes have been designed and built in Europe. However, Urbana has one climatic advantage over many cities in Germany that makes the design of a Passive House a bit easier. Urbana is at the same latitude as Rome, Italy, and has 4 times more solar radiation than, for example, Cologne, Germany. Taking all of these climate-related factors into account, Klingenberg determined that the Smith House required a superinsulated envelope on all six sides, with an R-value of at least 56 (R-56).

The foundation of the Smith House consists of a concrete block frost wall surrounding a floating 4-inch concrete slab, which was left exposed on the interior for thermal storage. The wall is insulated around the perimeter with 6 inches of expanded polystyrene (EPS), with another 14 inches of EPS under the slab. EPS was chosen over extruded polystyrene (XPS) because the expansion agent used in XPS at that time depleted the ozone layer and contributed to global warming. All available research showed that EPS would perform appropriately below grade.

The walls of the envelope are balloon framed, using 12-inch TJIs to achieve a 12-inch cavity in one framing step. That cavity is filled with 12 inches of high-density blown-in fiberglass insulation. An interior, structurally required sheathing layer of oriented strand board (OSB) serves as an airtight layer as well as a vapor barrier. OSB

The finished concrete floor is stylish, durable, low-maintenance, affordable—and it readily absorbs wintertime's warming solar radiation.

has a permeability (perm) rating of below 1, which is why it qualifies as a vapor barrier. In addition, the Smith House is wrapped on four sides in two 2-inch layers of EPS, with the joints staggered. Another layer of 1-inch by 4-inch pine strapping creates a vent space, which doubles as a rain screen façade underneath the final layer of cedar lap siding. The roof framing consists of 16-inch TJIs filled with high-density fiberglass insulation, topped by a vented metal roof.

Thermal bridging has been completely avoided, and there are no penetrations through the exterior envelope. Utilities and ducts enter the house from under the slab. Exterior nonconditioned structures and decks are structurally independent of the main house to eliminate thermal bridging, and are secured by anchors and bolts.

All of the windows are triple pane, argon filled, with various low-e coatings. The insulated fiberglass window frames contribute to the overall thermal performance of the walls. All windows and doors have multipoint locks to ensure that they seal tightly when they are closed. Their overall airtightness was checked during the blower-door test and found to be superior. With an R-value of between 6 and 8, all the windows, even the ceiling-height, south-facing ones, have a sufficiently warm inner surface to eliminate drafts caused by convection—so there is no need to place a heat source or supply vent directly under the window.

In winter, when the windows in the Smith House remain closed and the mechanical ventilation is working, one thing is noticeably absent: stratification. Temperatures on the second floor of the Smith House were measured in the winter and found to be lower than temperatures on the first floor. This is the opposite of what happens in most conventionally built homes, and what one would expect, given that hot air rises. In the Smith House, and in Passive Houses generally, air mixes very slowly and evenly. As a result, surface temperatures throughout are also even, which helps to reduce stratification.

Ducts and Pipes

The central component of the mechanical system is an HRV with a heat recovery efficiency of 90% and a very energy-efficient fan motor. This particular European ventilation unit has a computer-controlled summer bypass for in-between seasons when heat recovery isn't desired. It exchanges the air in the house at a constant low flow rate that is delivered to the bedrooms and living rooms, and exhausted from the kitchen and bathrooms, through a minimized duct system consisting of 6-inch trunk lines and 4-inch branch lines, with strategically placed sound mufflers. The ventilation system has a 1,000W electric-resistance heater integrated into the airstream, so no conventional heating system is needed to deliver conditioned air. All additional heating is provided by electric-resistance heat, including an in-floor electric-resistance heater in the bathroom as a point heat source for comfort.

Electric-resistance heat is a poor ecological choice; it is therefore not generally recommended for Passive Houses. There are such large efficiency losses during production and delivery of electricity that is generated off site that roughly 3 units of source energy must be generated for

The Smith House by the Numbers

Here are the final results of the PHPP 2007 calculations for the Smith House:

- specific heating energy requirement: 8 kWh/m²a (2.5 kBtu/ft²/yr);
- whole-house specific primary energy requirement: 111 kWh/m²a (35.2 kBtu/ft²/yr);
- peak heating load: 13.1 W/m² (4.2 Btu/h/ft²)
- airtightness: 0.6 ACH_{50}; and
- surface area-to-volume ratio (A/V): 0.74.

each 1 unit of electricity that is used on site. Klingenberg chose electric-resistance heat to meet the extremely low annual heating demand of 8 kWh/m² because its installation cost is less than all other options, and because she wanted to keep the mechanical system simple for the first prototype. She would have preferred to use a renewable heat source if she could have.

The air intake for the ventilation system is a 100-foot earth tube 8 inches in diameter; it is buried 6 feet underground. The earth tube slopes away from the house at a minimum drop of 2% and drains toward the cleanout, where any condensation is pumped out of the system. The earth tube intake has a filter to keep out organic matter. Earth tubes, whether for intake or for exhaust, do not penetrate the envelope; they enter and leave the house from under the slab, and so do not act as a thermal bridge. The earth tube prewarms the incoming air in the winter to above-freezing temperatures; the ventilator needs no additional freeze protection. In the summer, the earth tube precools and dehumidifies the incoming air, which has kept the house comfortable enough to live in without any mechanical air conditioning.

Domestic hot water (DHW) in the Smith House is provided by a tankless electric water heater. In the future, this heater will be supplemented by a solar-thermal system to further reduce energy consumption.

Penetrations are kept to an absolute minimum in the Smith House. Electrical installations, switches, and outlets along exterior walls are all surface mounted or located in the floor to avoid penetrations through the exterior airtight layer. Spare conduits for a future PV system come into the house from underneath the slab. There is a separate electric panel, with an emergency shutoff to and from the grid, as required by the local utility for net metering.

The vent stack of the plumbing system is capped in the attic with an air admittance valve. This is a small vacuum cap that allows air to enter the vent stack only when the plumbing is in use. The cap then closes and seals the vent stack to prevent sewer gases from

Project Data and Specifications of the Smith House

Location	Urbana, Illinois
Region and climate	*Latitude:* 40°6'57" *Longitude:* 88°14'34" *Elevation:* 738 ft Cold climate
Heating degree-days/ cooling degree-days	6,359/888
Year of construction	2002-2003
Typology	Single-family residence
Finished floor area	111 m² (1,200 ft², including double story space)
Owner/Designer	Katrin Klingenberg/Nicolas Smith
Builder	Edward Sindelar, Chicago
Energy Consultant	Conservation Technologies Duluth, Minnesota
Foundation	Concrete block frost wall
Foundation perimeter insulation	152 mm (6 in) of expanded polystyrene
Under-slab insulation	356 mm (14 in) of expanded polystyrene
Wall framing	Vertical 305 mm (12 in) TJIs
Wall insulation	305 mm (12 in) blown-in fiberglass plus 4 inches exterior rigid polystyrene
Roof framing	406 mm (16 in) TJIs with vent channels above the sheathing
Roof insulation	406 mm (16 in) blown-in fiberglass
Windows	Fiberglass frames with expanded polystyrene insulation, triple-pane glazing with super-spacers, argon-filled, low-e glazing, 0.61 SHGC south facing, 0.37 all other orientations, average overall U-value of frame and glazing: 1.09 W/(m²K)
Ventilation system	90% sensible efficiency HRV
Heating system	1,000W (3,400 Btu/h) electric-resistance element in the HRV, 100 ft earth tube, 40 ft² in-floor electrical radiant heating
DHW system	Tankless electric water heater, with spare conduit for later solar thermal addition

Active System requirement to become *net zero site energy*
2 kW photovoltaic system (not installed but wired in)*

Active System requirement to become *net zero source energy*
4.5 kW photovoltaic system (not installed but wired in)**

Active System requirement to become *plus energy/ carbon neutral*
5 kW photovoltaic system (not installed but wired in)***

* *Net zero site energy use:* In this type of building, the amount of energy provided by on-site renewable energy sources is equal to the amount of energy used by the building.

** *Net zero source energy use:* This type of building generates an amount of energy that is equivalent to the total amount of energy used both in the building and in transporting energy to the building, including the losses incurred during electricity transmission.

*** *Net zero energy emissions:* This type of building is also known as a plus energy, carbon neutral, zero carbon, or zero emissions building. To qualify for this label, the amount of on-site renewable energy production must balance out the carbon emissions generated from on-site or off-site fossil fuel use. Other definitions include not only the carbon emissions generated by using energy in the building, but also those generated in the construction of the building and the embodied energy of the structure.

escaping into the attic. The use of an air admittance valve makes it unnecessary to install a vent stack above the roof, which would require a penetration. An above-roof vent stack would also have to be insulated to prevent it conducting heat or cold from the outside to the home's interior. However, only a few state plumbing codes allow the use of this valve.

Comparing Costs

The total construction cost for the Smith House was $145,000. It is difficult to compare this cost with the cost of conventional construction. Here are some of the questions that need to be considered:

- What is the standard that Passive House construction is being compared to? Is it being compared to existing building stock, or to International Energy Conservation Code (IECC) 2006?

- Is it conditioned floor space or exterior dimensions that are being compared?

- How experienced are the planners and builders with nontraditional construction methods?

- Has Passive House design been integrated into the planning from the beginning? Or is the designer trying to tweak an existing design to meet Passive House standards—generally a more expensive proposition?

- How are projected energy savings being factored into the equation?

There are always costs associated with building differently. Experience has shown that the first estimated prices from subcontractors are usually higher than they need to be, just because the subcontractors don't really know what the job will cost and so they pad their estimates to cover any unexpected costs. Once the planner and builder have a couple of successful projects under their belt, and the subcontractors know what to expect, this learning cost decreases significantly, and with it, the overall cost per square foot.

Finally, when comparing the costs of conventionally built homes and Passive Houses, there is a need to distinguish between costs associated with energy efficiency features and costs associated with green features. Energy-efficient construction costs less than building green. Insulation, a mainstay of efficient homes, is the cheapest material on site. Reducing the mechanical system and ductwork saves money, offsetting much of the additional cost of extra insulation and better installation practices. Among all the components that contribute to increasing the efficiency of a home's thermal envelope, better windows and doors are the features that cost the most. In a green-built home, many types of standard construction materials are typically replaced, and often these increased costs exceed the costs of energy efficiency features. For example, vinyl siding is usually not used in a green home, because of concerns with its environmental impacts. Replacing vinyl siding with fiber cement siding can be a costly proposition, depending on the size of the house. Construction costs for a house built to both Passive House and green standards will be significantly higher than construction costs for a house built to Passive House standards alone.

The Smith House was the first Passive House that Klingenberg designed, and the first Passive House that the builder, Edward Sindelar, built. In the Urbana area at the time, standard construction cost, which usually is estimated using exterior dimensions of the home, in the area started at $70 to $90 per square foot. Construction quality delivered for the lowest price was truly low. Exterior walls were built from 2 x 3 studs and had almost no insulation, and the houses were vinyl sided. Construction cost for the Smith House, using exterior dimensions, was $94 per square foot. The Smith House saves 90% in operational energy over a standard house. For Klingenberg, these savings alone would justify the additional cost of constructing the Smith House, but they are just a small part of the many benefits that building and living in a Passive House brings.

For more information:

To learn about the **Smith House**, go to
www.e-colab.org/ecolab/SmithHouse.html.

Chapter 3
The Waldsee BioHaus

Architect Stephan Tanner designed the BioHaus to showcase German architectural trends and American home-building products.

Completed in 2006, the Waldsee BioHaus, in Bemidji, Minnesota, was the first officially certified Passive House in the United States. (The Smith House, which was completed three years earlier, was recognized by Dr. Feist at the time as meeting the Passive House standard, as we explained in chapter 2, but it was not officially certified.) Commissioned by the Concordia Language Villages, the BioHaus functions as an educational and environmental living center for Concordia's German-language and cultural immersion programs.

Architect Stephan Tanner designed the BioHaus to showcase German architectural trends and American home-building products. Most of the building's components are manufactured, and are widely available, in the United States. A few building components were imported from Germany to ensure that the building would meet the requirements of the Passive House standard. These imported components include the technologically advanced insulation, the high-performance windows, the air-handling equipment with its high-efficiency plate heat exchanger, and a ground-to-air heat exchanger.

The BioHaus design concept was inspired by the vision of immersion learning, which honors the unique perspectives of different cultures. The BioHaus takes a German perspective on

the relationship between nature and the built environment. It does so by exploring three themes—the themes of *Durchblick, Ausblick, and Einblick.*

Durchblick means perspective, vista, or view in German, but it also means seeing through something. Forest is the main natural element in northern Minnesota, and the BioHaus is designed to fit almost seamlessly into this element. You walk through a forest to enter the BioHaus, and upon entering, you feel as if you were still in the forest, because you can see through the building to more forest on the other side.

Ausblick means perspective or vista in German, but it also connotes seeing into the future. The large windows to the south give a sense of perspective to the students using the common room or the studio, creating a fitting environment for learning, and for shaping their futures.

Einblick means insight in German, and it also connotes seeing into or inspecting. The small window to the west in the studio symbolizes this, by casting light on the place where students can learn about the environment.

Functionally, the design of the BioHaus consists of two elements—the private areas and the public areas. The private areas, which contain the dormitories and a staff apartment, are housed on the ground floor toward the rear of the building. Massive blue stucco walls give these areas a sense of security and sheltering. Aluminum siding and thinner walls give a lighter, more reflective feeling to the public areas—areas intended for learning, playing, and holding meetings.

A High-Performance Building Envelope

Constructing a Passive House in the challenging climate of Bemidji, where winter temperatures stay below zero for weeks at a time, requires careful attention to every aspect of the building, starting with its shape. Buildings with a low surface-to-volume ratio take up the least land and need the least energy to heat and cool. To minimize the environmental impact of the BioHaus, Tanner designed it as a two-story building with a nearly square footprint—54 feet by 51 feet. With its thick exterior walls, the interior living space measures just under 5,000 square feet.

Given Minnesota's cold winters, it was critical to insulate all parts of the building envelope. Specific attention was paid to insulating under the slab. This was done by installing rigid insulation to give the slab an R-value of 55. All the below-grade exterior walls were built with insulated concrete blocks and an exterior insulation and finish system (EIFS), which together gave these walls an R-value of 55. The above-grade exterior walls were standard wood frame construction, insulated to an R-value of 70, using a

The **BioHaus** takes a German perspective on the relationship between **nature** and the **built environment**.

Cal Rice

water-based foam (Icynene) in combination with an exterior insulation. Windows and doors have an R-value of 8. All of the above-grade walls were coated on the outside with a spray-on waterproofing, which acts as an air barrier that is vapor permeable.

The second-story exterior walls and the lower roof structure were insulated with VIPs, a more advanced insulation technology. The R-value of a VIP is approximately 10 times that of most standard insulation materials—R-30 as compared to R-3.5 per inch. The VIPs used at the BioHaus are 2 inches thick. They were used to replace 16 inches of standard insulation, thereby reducing the thickness of the walls and the lower roof structure by 14 inches. The VIPs were placed over a layer of 2-inch rigid foam board and covered by another layer of rigid foam board to complete the roof assembly. The foam board serves to protect the VIPs from any sort of accidental penetration, and to minimize thermal bridging. In addition to this insulation layer, there is 12 inches of foam insulation between the roof joists. This gives the lower roof structure a total R-value of 100. The upper roof, which is insulated between the trusses and a row of perpendicular sleeper trusses

with 28 inches of foam insulation, also has a total R-value of 100.

The roof was designed to accommodate what is known as a green roof—essentially a roof that can be planted in vegetation. In the summer, this vegetation retains rainwater and reduces runoff in the surrounding landscape. The soil and vegetation together also create a heat buffer, helping to keep the building cool on hot summer days. In winter, the flat roof accumulates snow, which acts as an additional insulation blanket on the roof.

High-performance windows complete the high-performance building envelope. The performance of many building products often depends heavily on the skills of the installer. This is certainly true when it comes to windows. For the BioHaus, German manufacturer Müller Fensterbau donated Passivhaus-certified Optiwin-brand 3wood windows. These are argon-filled, triple-pane windows, whose frame contains an inner layer of structural wood, cork insulation, and an outer layer of larch wood. Klaus Müller, one of the company partners, came from Germany with one of his employees to install them properly.

Proper installation included the following steps. First, each frame was set temporarily into its rough opening to determine overall fit, and to take measurements, especially for the corners. Next, each frame was set on sawhorses, and double-sided butyl tape was applied around all four sides to create an airtight seal between the window frame and the rough opening. The taped frame was then placed in the opening, shimmed, and eventually screwed into place. Foam insulation was sprayed from the outside into the space between the wall and the frame, to minimize thermal bridging. Last of all, the glass was installed in the frame.

Rooms that are much used during the day, such as the common room and the studio, need the best access to daylighting. Accordingly, Tanner located those rooms upstairs on the south side of the building, where most of the windows in the building are located. There are additional transom windows on the north wall of the building for daylighting and natural ventilation. Dormitories, which are used mostly in the early morning and at night, are located on the lower level, on the east side of the building, and most of the windows in those rooms face east. The bedrooms in the staff apartment on the upper level face north, while the living and dining rooms face east. Solar blinds for the south-facing windows came from the German manufacturer Warema. Service areas—the toilet rooms and showers—which don't need any windows, are compact and centrally located, to minimize plumbing runs.

The PHI requires that buildings pass a stringent blower door test to be eligible for Passivhaus certification. Passive Houses built in the United States must meet the same requirement. Gary Nelson, who helped pioneer blower door testing in the 1980s, and

who is now president of the Energy Conservatory, a manufacturer of blower doors and other diagnostic equipment, came to Waldsee to conduct the test personally. The results—just 0.18 ACH_{50}—show how thoroughly the builder and his crew worked to make the envelope airtight. To achieve this level of airtightness, a Passive House designer must have a clear air-sealing strategy, a clear understanding of construction management, clear expectations for the installing trades, and comprehensive oversight. The airtightness level of the BioHaus is 2½ times better than the Passivhaus standard—and approximately 20 times better than the current Minnesota standard. Gary Nelson has performed hundreds of these tests, and he says that the BioHaus is one of the tightest U.S. buildings he has ever tested.

Passive House–Appropriate Technologies

The BioHaus has a very efficient ventilation system— one that provides plenty of fresh air at all times. During the winter and summer, the incoming fresh air passes first through almost 330 feet of antimicrobial earth tubes buried 8 to 9 feet underground. These tubes function as a ground-to-air heat exchange system. The air then passes through an 85% efficient HRV. In cold weather, this HRV extracts the heat from the exhaust air and transfers it to the incoming air. On a day when the outside temperature is −32°F, for example, the incoming

Project Data and Specifications of the Waldsee BioHaus

Location	Bemidji, Minnesota
Region and climate	*Latitude:* 47°28'14" N *Longitude:* 94°52'39" W *Elevation:* 1,350 ft Very cold climate
Heating degree-days/ cooling degree-days	9,869/296
Year of construction	2006
Typology	School building
Finished floor area	401.3 m² (4,320 ft²)
Owner	Concordia Language Village
Architect	Stephan Tanner, AIA
Foundation	330 mm (13 in) ICFs; 203 mm (8 in) EIFS
Foundation perimeter insulation	N/A
Under-slab insulation	406 mm (16 in) rigid insulation
Wall framing	*Wall type 1:* 2 x 12 stud wall 24 in OC *Wall type 2:* 2 x 6 stud wall 24 in OC
Wall insulation	*Wall type 1:* 286 mm (11.25 in) water-based spray foam insulation; 203-mm (8 in) EIFS *Wall type 2:* 140 mm (5.25 in) water-based spray foam insulation; 51-mm (2-in) VIPs

Roof framing	*Lower roof:* 305 mm (11 7/8 in) TJIs *Upper roof:* 305 mm (11 7/8 in) TJIs with 203 mm (8 in) perpendicular sleeper trusses
Roof insulation	*Lower roof:* 305 mm (11 7/8 in) water-based spray foam insulation, 51 mm (2 in) VIPs *Upper roof:* 711 mm (28 in) water-based spray foam insulation
Windows	Optiwin Passivhaus-certified, 3Wood windows; pine structural frame, cork insulation, larch outer layer; low-e, argon-filled, triple-pane glazing; average overall U-value of frame and glazing: 0.79 W/(m²K) (0.14 Btu/[h ft² F])
Ventilation system	85% efficient HRV
Heating system	19,400 Btu/h ground source heat pump
DHW system	19.8 m² (213 ft²) solar flat-plate collectors for DHW and hydronic in-floor heat

Active System requirement to become *net zero site energy* 3.5 kW PV system (not installed but wired in)

Active System requirement to become *net zero source energy* 9.2 kW PV system (not installed but wired in)

Active System requirement to become *plus energy/carbon neutral* 10.8 kW PV system (not installed but wired in)

Active System desired, which will produce more than enough energy to make BioHaus *plus energy/ carbon neutral* 25 kW PV system (not installed but wired in) fresh air is warmed to 58°F by these passive means. The residual energy needed to meet the building's annual heating requirement of 4,350 Btu/ft^2 is supplied by a ground source heat pump and passive-solar gain. During the spring and fall seasons, when the temperatures are milder, the windows can be flung open and the ventilation system can be shut off.

Although all residents are asked to conserve hot water, shower times are not limited. The sometimes high demand for hot water is met with a solar-powered water heating system, with the ground source heat pump as a backup.

The only energy source for the BioHaus is electricity. At present, this electricity comes from the grid. A PV system will be installed when financing becomes available. This system will generate more electricity than the BioHaus uses, making the house plus energy and carbon neutral.

The sometimes high demand for hot water is met with a solar-powered water heating system, which juts up from the flat roof. A ground source heat pump acts as a backup.

The BioHaus by the Numbers

Here are the final results of the PHPP 2004 calculations for the Waldsee BioHaus:

- *specific heating energy requirement:*
  13.7 kWh/m^{2}a (4.35 kBtu/ft^2/yr);
  specific primary energy requirement:
  83 kWh/m^{2}a (26.3 kBtu/ft^2/yr);
  Peak heating load: 16.9 W/m^2 (5.4 Btu/h/ft^2)
  airtightness: 0.18 ACH$_{50}$; and
  surface area-to-volume ratio (A/V): 0.68.

Guaranteeing IAQ

An efficient ventilation system does not in itself guarantee good IAQ, since the house and its furnishings may generate more pollutants than the system can filter out. To achieve the best possible IAQ, Tanner specified low-emitting building products and materials. This strategy—which also serves to meet regulatory requirements—is especially important when designing spaces to be used by children, who are sensitive to environmental contaminants, and who are developing allergies and other chronic illnesses at increasing rates, partly in response to exposure to these contaminants.

To achieve the best possible IAQ, Tanner specified

- fungicide-, insecticide-, and bactericide-free interior materials and finishes;
- formaldehyde-free or low-formaldehyde interior finishes;
- low volatile organic compound (low-VOC) adhesives, paints, and other chemicals; and
- no chemical wood preservatives, except where required by code.

Choosing Sustainability

At all times, Tanner strove to minimize the environmental impact of the BioHaus, and to make the most efficient use of building materials and other resources. To this end, he set the following requirements:

- Choose renewable or mineral-based materials and products for finishes.
- Choose local or regional resources that can be sustainably harvested or manufactured.
- Use materials and products with recycled content whenever possible.
- Avoid using tropical wood for construction and cabinetry.
- Choose inert building materials and products that can be recycled or reused when the building is deconstructed.

- Avoid using ozone-depleting building materials and refrigerating agents.
- Avoid using chlorofluorocarbon (CFC)-based expansion foams, adhesives, and insulating materials.
- Avoid using halogenated CFC refrigerating agents, cleaning agents, solvents, and extinguishing devices.
- Minimize the building's primary energy demand and subsequent emissions of carbon dioxide (CO_2) and sulfur dioxide (SO_2).

Architect's Vision: Stephan Tanner

By paying thorough attention to all aspects of the BioHaus's environmental footprint—from energy use to IAQ to its impact on the environment over time—Tanner and the entire construction crew created a building that will comfortably and efficiently house its residents for generations to come. But the building does more than shelter those who live there. It is also a learning tool for the many students who enroll in Concordia's language and cultural immersion programs. Tanner hopes that the comfort they experience at BioHaus will help shape their expectations for their own homes.

For more information:

To find out more about the **Waldsee BioHaus**, or to find out how you can visit it, go to **www.waldseebiohaus.typepad.com**.

Chapter 4
The Fairview Houses

K atrin Klingenberg and her team designed e-co lab's first project, Fairview House I, to demonstrate that Passive Houses could be built for low-income, first-time home buyers at a price they could afford. But the project was more than just a demonstration. E-co lab's mission is to provide superefficient housing to the people who are hit hardest by escalating energy and housing costs. The first Fairview House was eventually sold to a woman who had been displaced from her home in New Orleans by Hurricane Katrina. Construction has now been completed on Fairview II, which refines and improves upon Fairview I.

Fairview I

The Site

In the progressive city of Urbana, Illinois, e-co lab found a formidable ally. Wanting to support the lab's mission of providing superefficient and affordable housing, Urbana donated the land on which Fairview I was built. The large lot, which had been vacant for over 20 years, was situated on the south side of the street. One big tree on the south end of the lot would provide shading in summer. In winter, when the tree drops its leaves, the future home would receive ample sunlight through its south-facing windows.

Mike Kernagis braces the large truss joist I-beam framing members during construction of the exterior envelope of Fairview I.

The Structure

Fairview I is a three-bedroom, two-bathroom house with a finished floor area of 1,350 square feet. Construction began in February 2006 and was completed in October 2006. The design is straightforward; the house forms a compact rectangle, with a two-story space over the entry, kitchen, and dining areas. The house rests on a thickened-edge slab 35 feet by 25 feet. There is 16 inches of EPS under the slab itself, 4 inches of high-density XPS under the 24-inch thickened edge, and 2¾ inches of XPS around the perimeter of the slab. Two feet of lateral frost skirt protection, provided by a 2-inch layer of XPS, makes possible a thickened edge that is relatively shallow—just 20 inches deep—for east-central Illinois.

The walls of Fairview I are constructed of 14-inch TJIs; the sills and top plates are 1¼-inch laminated-strand lumber. TJIs, which are usually used as floor joists, are used here in an upright application at 24 inches OC. The walls were balloon framed on site and were raised with the help of a crane. The interior side of the TJIs is sheathed with OSB, which serves as both an air and vapor barrier. The joints of the OSB are sealed with urethane glue. The exterior side of the TJIs is sheathed with structural fiberboard, which is vapor permeable, allowing moisture to pass out of the wall. With these sheathings, the walls of Fairview

I resemble a box beam, and they have a comparable structural integrity.

The thickness of the walls in a Passive House depends on the climate in which it is built. Since the design temperatures range from –10°F to 95°F in this part of Illinois, the 14-inch walls of Fairview I are filled with high-density blown-in fiberglass, for an R-value of around 60. Similarly, the harsh conditions here call for more substantial windows than would be needed in a milder climate. For Fairview I, Klingenberg specified argon-filled, triple-pane, low-e windows with insulated fiberglass frames, to eliminate thermal bridging. The cost of these windows ate a sizable hole in the budget, but they were essential for reducing heat loss through the entire wall assembly.

Determined to ensure that the building would last as long as possible, Klingenberg spared little expense on exterior finishes that would protect it from the weather. The siding is durable fiber cement planking. Furring strips between the exterior sheathing and the fiber cement planking create a cavity that acts as a rain screen. The cavity also provides convective cooling in the summer.

The roof is framed with 16-inch TJIs set 24 inches OC, forming a vaulted ceiling. The roof is sheathed with fiberboard on the exterior and with gypsum board on the interior, with 16 inches of high-density fiberglass blown in between the joists, giving it an R-value of about 75. A layer of 6-mil polyethylene plastic is installed between the roof framing and the interior sheathing; it serves as an air and vapor barrier. This barrier is taped and sealed to the interior wall sheathing to create a continuous airtight envelope. On the exterior, the roof decking is furred out, creating another venting space. The roofing is standing-seam metal with concealed fasteners.

Mechanical System

Constant, balanced, fresh-air ventilation is provided by a 95% efficient ERV and a very simple duct system supplying the living room and bedrooms, with returns located in the kitchen and baths. Humidity sensors, located at the returns, trigger the ERV to increase its rate of flow when the humidity in these rooms exceeds 40%. In winter, when the temperature outdoors drops below 10°F, a simple electric-coil preheater on a thermostat warms incoming fresh air before it enters the ERV. This prevents the ERV from freezing up. What little mechanical space heating the home requires is supplied by a handful of small and seldom-used electric-resistance

One big tree on the south end provides **shading in summer**. **In winter**, when the tree **drops its leaves,** the home receives **ample sunlight** through its south-facing windows.

baseboard heaters. The house also has an electric on-demand water heater, which heats water only when it is needed. Using electricity for space and water heating is not ideal in Illinois, where most electricity is generated with coal, but the budgetary constraints of low-income construction precluded more elegant options on this project.

The differences between the heating system of a Passive House and that of a standard-built house lead to crucial differences in the cost of those systems. The few 500W baseboard heaters installed at Fairview I cost a mere $30 apiece, and were installed quickly and easily. By comparison, a heating system in a standard-built house generally costs about 2½ times as much as the ERV, ductwork, and baseboard heaters combined, including all the installations. The difference goes a long way toward offsetting the added costs for insulation, windows, and air sealing in a Passive House.

Performance

A blower door test, administered by the Building Research Council at the University of Illinois Urbana-Champaign, revealed that Fairview I is quite tight—just 0.24 ACH_{50}. This level of airtightness, well below the required 0.6 ACH_{50}, contributes greatly to the energy performance of the house. Achieving such a tight structure meant avoiding unnecessary penetrations of the envelope. All of the wiring enters from below the

The north side of Fairview I was designed to have very small windows as it has no winter solar gain.

Fairview I by the Numbers

Here are the final results of the PHPP 2004 calculations for the Fairview I House:

- *specific heating energy requirement:* 14.4 kWh/m²a (4.6 kBtu/ft²/yr);
- *specific cooling energy requirement not calculated in PHPP 2004;*
- *specific primary energy requirement:* 120 kWh/m²a (38 kBtu/ft²/yr);
- *peak heating load:* 16.1 W/m² (5.1 Btu/h/ft²);
- *airtightness:* 0.24 ACH_{50}; and
- *surface area-to-volume ratio (A/V):* 0.79.

Project Data and Specifications of Fairview I

Location	Urbana, Illinois	**Roof framing**	406 mm (16 inches) TJIs with fiberboard sheathing
Region and climate	*Latitude:* 40°6'57" *Longitude:* 88°14'34" *Elevation:* 738 ft Cold climate	**Roof insulation**	406 mm (16 in) blown-in cellulose
Heating degree-days/ cooling degree-days	6,359/888	**Windows**	Fiberglass frames with EPS insulation; triple-pane glazing with superspacers, argon-filled, low-e glazing, 0.56 SHGC south facing, 0.33 all other orientations; average overall U-value of frame and glazing: 1.09 W/(m^{2}K) (0.19 Btu/[h ft^2 F])
Year of construction	2006		
Typology	Single-family residence		
Finished floor area	125.4 m^2 (1,350 ft^2, including 2-story space)	**Ventilation system**	95% sensible efficiency ERV
Owner	Elisabeth Simpson	**Heating system**	5 x 500W electric-resistance baseboard heaters
Designer/Builder	Ecological Construction Laboratory	**DHW system**	Tankless electric water heater
Foundation	Thickened-edge slab on 102 mm (4 in) high-density XPS		
Foundation perimeter insulation	51 mm (2 in) XPS		
Under-slab insulation	406 mm (16 in) EPS		
Wall framing	Vertical 356-mm (14 in) TJIs		
Wall insulation	356 mm (14 in) high-density blown-in fiberglass		

Active System requirement to become *net zero site energy*
2.5 kW PV system (not installed but wired in)

Active System requirement to become *net zero source energy*
5.9 kW PV system (not installed but wired in)

Active System requirement to become *plus energy/ carbon neutral*
6.9 kW PV system (not installed but wired in)

slab and passes through surface-mounted raceways, in order to not penetrate the airtight layer. The plumbing also enters from below the slab, and all plumbing is located in one interior wall between the kitchen and bath; this eliminates thermal bridging, as well as the possibility of air leaks.

One of e-co lab's primary goals in building Fairview I was to generate monitoring data to show how a Passive House performs in, for example, Illinois and how much energy it takes to heat and cool such a house. Integrated Building and Construction Solutions (IBACOS), a partner in DOE's Building America program, is helping e-co lab to compile these data. Portable data-logging sensors that monitor temperature and humidity were distributed throughout the house, in the ventilator, and outside. Temperature, humidity, and moisture content sensors were placed at several points across the gradient of the wall structure. The ventilator, its preheater, the baseboard heaters, the water heater, and the range are all separately monitored. As of this writing, monitoring data have not yet been compiled.

E-co lab estimates that the construction cost of Fairview I was 10% higher than that of a comparable conventional house in Urbana.

Fairview II

Having proven with Fairview I that a house for low-income buyers could be built that would meet such an impressive standard, e-co lab now set out to improve upon this model. Despite the obvious advantages of such an efficient home, the upfront cost was still slightly higher than that of a conventional house—an obstacle for first-time home buyers on limited budgets. How could construction be made faster and cheaper without sacrificing the high-quality building practices needed to achieve the Passive House standard? Prefabrication was the answer.

The Site
The city of Urbana, pleased with the success of the first Fairview project, donated the adjacent vacant lot to e-co lab. Though identical in size to the first, this lot had two large evergreen trees on the south side. Fortunately, a sun-tracking analysis showed that the trees would not reduce solar heat gain appreciably in the winter.

Thanks to its prefabricated superinsulated wall panels, Fairview II progressed from flat slab to roofed and wrapped—roof sheathing, roofing paper, and house wrap all installed—in a day and a half.

The Structure

Built between August 2007 and January 2008, Fairview II has many of the same elements as its predecessor: a well-insulated thickened-edge slab; a simple rectangular footprint 35 feet by 25 feet; and a compact two-story structure with an attached garage. The walls, like those of Fairview I, were built of balloon-framed TJIs, sheathed on the inside with OSB and on the outside with structural fiberboard. But in an important departure, the walls of Fairview II were prefabricated.

Months before construction began, e-co lab went to work developing shop drawings of the wall panels—16 two-story superinsulated panels, each one about 18 feet high, 8 feet wide, and 12 inches thick. The drawings were shown to several prefab framers, who expressed little interest in this unfamiliar concept. However, e-co lab persisted. Eventually it found a team from a nearby Amish community who were willing to fabricate and assemble the panels. Fabrication was coordinated with the insulation contractor, who blew 12 inches of high-density fiberglass into the wall panels at the fabrication shop. Again, 1¼-inch laminated-strand lumber was used for the plates, and structural fiberboard was employed as an exterior sheathing. Since the interior side was once again sheathed with OSB, which would serve as an air and vapor barrier, it was glued and screwed to the TJIs. This ensured that the panel would be airtight. Transported to the site, the tall panels were set in place with an end loader, and the panels were lifted by means of temporarily attached hooks. Then the panels were glued together at overlapping joints. The Amish crew also built a prefabricated roof truss system, with raised heels to allow for adequate insulation at the eaves.

Project Data and Specifications of Fairview II

Location	Urbana, Illinois
Region and climate	*Latitude:* 40°6'57" *Longitude:* 88°14'34" *Elevation:* 738 ft Cold climate
Heating degree-days/ cooling degree-days	6,359/888
Year of construction	2007–2008
Typology	Single-family residence
Finished floor area	123 m² (1,325 ft²)
Owner	Ecological Construction Laboratory
Designer/Builder	Ecological Construction Laboratory
Foundation	Thickened-edge slab on 102 mm (4 in) high-density XPS
Foundation perimeter insulation	51 mm (2 in) XPS
Under-slab insulation	406 mm (16 in) EPS
Wall framing	Vertical 305-mm (12 in) TJls; interior 2 x 4 stud wall
Wall insulation	305 mm (12 in) blown-in fiberglass; 89 mm (3½ in) blown-in fiberglass
Roof framing	Prefabricated wood trusses with vent chutes underneath the sheathing; interior 2 x 4 stud
Roof insulation	508 mm (20 in) blown-in cellulose; 89 mm (3½ in) blown-in fiberglass
Windows	Fiberglass frames with EPS insulation; triple-pane glazing with superspacers, argon-filled, low-e glazing, 0.61 SHGC south facing, 0.37 all other orientations; average overall U-value of frame and glazing: 1.09 W/(m²K) (0.19 Btu/[h ft² F])
Ventilation system	95% sensible efficiency ERV
Heating system	9,000 Btu/h 20 SEER mini-split air-to-air heat pump for heating and cooling; 5 x 500W electric-resistance baseboard heaters
DHW system	5.4 m² solar flat-plate collectors with tankless electric water heater for backup (not yet installed)

Active System requirement to become *net zero site energy*
1.5 kW PV system (not installed but wired in)

Active System requirement to become *net zero source energy* 3.5 kW PV system (not installed but wired in)

Active System requirement to become *plus energy/carbon neutral* 4.1 kW PV system (not installed but wired in)

Fairview II, like its predecessor next door, was built for a first-time, low-income home buyer.

Fairview II by the Numbers

Here are the final results of the PHPP 2007 calculations for the Fairview II House:

- *specific heating energy requirement:*
  13.7 kWh/m²a (4.35 kBtu/ft²/yr);
- *specific cooling energy requirement:*
  3 kWh/m²a (1kBtu/ft²/yr)
- *specific primary energy requirement:*
  83 kWh/m²a (26.3 kBtu/ft²/yr);
- *peak heating load:* 16 W/m² (5 Btu/h/ft²);
- *airtightness:* 0.4 ACH₅₀; and
- *surface area-to-volume ratio (A/V):* 0.79.

There were further improvements. The crew constructed a second wall inside the first wall. This second wall was built using 2-inch by 3-inch framing members placed 24 inches OC, and sheathed with gypsum board. This interior wall allowed for concealed electrical and plumbing runs inside the envelope, eliminating the need for penetrations in the prefabricated panels. The first-floor interior framing also served as a bearing wall for the upstairs flooring system. This wall was insulated with blown-in cellulose before the drywall was hung, bringing the total R-value for the double-walled assembly to R-60.

The more conventionally constructed roof system was insulated with 2 feet of loose-blown cellulose. This, combined with an insulated interior 2 x 3 ceiling similar in construction to the interior wall, gives a walloping total R-value of 101. E-co lab assumes that this R-value will decrease slightly as the loose cellulose settles over time. The increased insulation of Fairview II meant that less passive-solar energy would be needed to keep the house warm during the winter, so the designers were able to decrease the size of the south-facing windows, making them cheaper to buy and easier to install.

Refining on the layout of the house next door, e-co lab chose to build another bedroom in what had been the two-story space above the kitchen and dining rooms; Fairview II has four bedrooms and two baths. Together, the prefabricated components and the slightly simpler layout startlingly reduced construction time. Fairview II progressed from flat slab to roofed and wrapped—roof sheathing, roofing paper, and house wrap all installed—in a day and a half. It had taken Fairview I a couple of months to reach the same point.

Mechanical and Plumbing Systems

To provide fresh air, e-co lab used the same high-efficiency ERV that was used in Fairview I but relocated it to an upstairs closet, which created space for a pantry off the kitchen. E-co lab also chose to use the same electric on-demand water heater to supply DHW. As in Fairview I, all plumbing is located in one interior wall between the kitchen and bath. The second bath lies directly above the first, and the laundry is adjacent to the upstairs bath. This layout minimizes the runs for water lines, which reduces heat loss from these lines and improves the overall efficiency of the water heating system.

An important new feature of Fairview II is the efficient, 20 SEER mini-split heat pump. Popular in Europe and southeast Asia, the mini-split is a ductless heating-and-cooling system. It can also remove humidity, which, in the muggy summers of Illinois, is responsible for most of the latent cooling load. The mini-split has two main components: a compressor/condenser that sits on the ground outside and an air-handling unit that is mounted on an interior wall. To accommodate the line

set between the two, a well-sealed penetration of the envelope is required.

Performance

Despite the novelty of the panelized approach, scrupulous attention to air sealing enabled e-co lab to best the Passive House requirement of 0.6 ACH$_{50}$. The results of the blower door test on Fairview II came in at 0.45 ACH$_{50}$. E-co lab is confident that future Passive Houses built in this way will do even better.

Once again, IBACOS set up a number of systems to monitor performance. The exterior walls are being monitored across their thickness for temperature, moisture content, and relative humidity. Temperature and humidity sensors are located throughout the house and outside the house. There is even an exterior sunlight meter to capture annual insolation. The ERV, water heater, heat pump, and all other appliances—in fact, all the electrical circuits—are also wired for monitoring that can be conducted from IBACOS's offices in Pittsburgh, Pennsylvania. As of this writing, the house has yet to be occupied, so no hard data are available.

For more information:

To learn more about **the Fairview Houses,** visit **www.e-colab.org/ecolab/Projects.html**.

Chapter 5
The Cleveland Farm

The main house, with its 4,544 square feet of finished floor area, is nestled in the trees, and all the neighboring houses are hidden from view.

Cleveland Farm, a single-family residence and egg farm, is located on Martha's Vineyard, an island southeast of Boston, Massachusetts. The family bought the property in 2005, after living in Amsterdam, Netherlands, for seven years. Returning from Europe, they were looking to build a house that would be as energy efficient as ones that they had recently seen in Europe.

In March 2007, the family attended a Passive House workshop on the island. Inspired by how environmentally responsible Passive House design is, they made an ambitious decision. Not only would their home be energy efficient enough to meet the Passive House standard, but it would also produce more energy than it consumed, making their family energy independent. Energy on the island is an expensive commodity, since it has to be imported. To make their home energy independent, the family set themselves two goals. First, they would build their house to meet the Passive House standard. Second, they would install a 5kW wind turbine, which they expect will generate more energy than they need. If that is the case, they will sell the excess energy back to the utility company.

Four months after the family attended the workshop, construction began on the home. It was completed in September 2008. The turbine went up in late July 2008 and started generating electricity immediately. The envelope and the mechanical system were designed to meet the Passive House standard, with modeling input from the PHPP software. The family plan to get the house certified by the PHI and PHIUS.

Designing a Sustainable Lifestyle

The family's long-term goal for this rural site is to create an energy-independent, self-sufficient lifestyle, with a main house, a guest house, a pump house, a barn, and a wind turbine. The property is long and narrow—400 feet by 2,000 feet—with a driveway that winds along the northern edge of property, leading to the main house at the far eastern edge. The house is nestled in the trees, and all the neighboring houses are hidden from view. In addition to the family, 65 chickens are living on the land; their eggs are sold to local markets.

The layout of the site and all the buildings on it was planned with two goals in mind. First, the approach to the main house reveals a series of buildings and fields in a carefully planned sequence—a sequence that creates a visual narrative about living sustainably.

Second, each element of the site is placed in a way that takes into account its functionality, its relationship with adjacent buildings, its solar orientation, and the views from each building.

The first of these elements to be built was the main house, with its 4,544 square feet of finished floor area. The house has two faces, each with a different expression. The north and east face conveys both privacy and intrigue, with a long cascading roofline that becomes a shingled blanket of sorts. The small windows on the north and east face form a pattern that leads the eye around the house to what lies beyond—the second face.

Designing to meet strict **energy efficiency** requirements can be consistent with **capturing** the **best views,** and creating a very **aesthetically pleasing** home.

The expression of the south and west face is much more open. The big windows and glass doors maximize solar gain, and provide dramatic views down the site to the west. The wide roof overhangs shield the house from the summer sun, but also lead the eye away from the house toward the rest of the farm.

Making the Best of the Site

Boston-based architect Craig Buttner designed the main house and worked out its location on the site. At the point when PHIUS was brought in as a Passive House consultant, there was little room for major changes; the location of the house had already been decided, in keeping with the design goals described above; and its orientation had been determined by the views, which meant that most of the windows faced west. The design of the house is typical for New England; it is mostly compact, with a pitched roof, and a wing jutting off that contains the master bedroom suite and the study. Although the orientation and surface-to-volume ratio of the house are not ideal for meeting the Passive House standard, the house manages to meet this standard nevertheless. It shows that designing to meet strict energy efficiency requirements need not be inconsistent with capturing the best

views, or creating a very aesthetically pleasing home. Large overhangs on the windows will prevent unwanted solar gain in the summer and compensate for the large number of west-facing windows. The less-than-optimal surface-to-volume ratio, together with the relative lack of south-facing windows, creates a need for more insulation. There is 2 more inches of insulation in the envelope than would have been needed had the house had a more compact shape, and a better orientation.

Walls, Foundation, and Roof

The exterior wall is 12-inch double-stud construction, with the studs spaced 24 inches OC. It is sheathed on the exterior with plywood. A 2-inch layer of flash spray foam polyurethane was applied to the inside of the exterior sheathing to make this layer airtight. The remaining cavity was then filled with 4 lb/ft^2 (10 inches) of dense-packed cellulose. The interior sheathing is gypsum board installed in an airtight manner and finished with a continuous coat of plaster. Latex paint over the plaster acts as a vapor retarder on the inside. The wall has an overall R-value of 47.

Starting with the exterior, the roof assembly is constructed as follows: vented cedar shingle; a rubberized asphalt protective membrane for waterproofing; plywood sheathing; a 2-inch layer of spray foam polyurethane; 16-inch TJI roof joists placed 24 inches OC and the remaining cavity filled with dense-

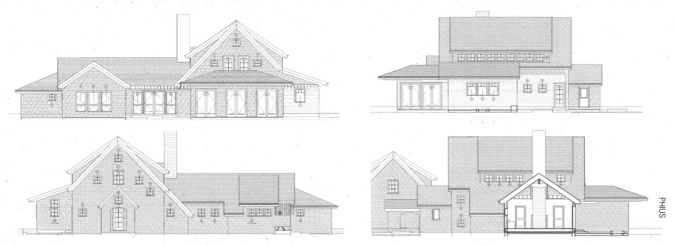

The design of the house is typical for New England; it is mostly compact, with a pitched roof, and a wing jutting off that contains the master bedroom suite and the study.

packed cellulose; and finally an airtight layer of gypsum board finished with a plaster coating and latex paint. The overall R-value of the roof is 61.

The basement wall assembly, starting with the exterior, is constructed as follows: 3 inches of XPS exterior insulation; liquid-applied membrane for waterproofing; a 10-inch-thick concrete foundation wall; 2 inches of spray foam polyurethane; a 2 x 4 stud wall filled with dense-packed cellulose; and again an airtight layer of gypsum board with a plaster coating and latex paint. The overall R-value of the basement wall is 35.

The basement slab is insulated under the concrete with 8 inches of EPS. Two inches of high-density EPS

were layered between the foundation wall and the edge of the slab, as a thermal break. The overall R-value of the slab is 34.

The slab-on-grade floor in the master wing, where there is no basement, is insulated with 2 inches of EPS on top of the slab. On top of the insulation is a built-up floor made of 12-inch TJI joists insulated with dense-packed cellulose. The joists are sheathed with ¾-inch tongue-and-groove OSB, with all the joints glued and sealed. The OSB doubles as a vapor barrier, since its perm rating is less than 1, and as an airtight layer. The overall R-value of the wing slab is 49. A vertical frost skirt consisting of 2 inches of XPS is applied around the perimeter of the wing, on the outside of the concrete slab, in continuation with the exterior insulation around the basement walls. This creates a continuous finish for the base of the whole house.

Eliminating Thermal Bridges

As in every house, there were many areas where thermal bridging might have been a problem, but in this house, all those areas were addressed. Because there were some large spans in the basement, some steel framing and steel columns were structurally necessary. Steel has a relatively high thermal conductivity, so all of the steel framing was thermally separated from the foundation wall and from any contact with the building envelope or with the outdoor temperature, by at least 2 inches of polyurethane foam. The rim joist areas on the first and second floor were filled with 10 inches of spray-on polyurethane. As explained above, the edge of the slab was isolated from the foundation wall by 2 inches of high-density EPS.

Before PHIUS was brought in, the design had included a traditional masonry fireplace with a footing in the basement. PHIUS promptly eliminated this fireplace, since the chimney created an easy thermal connection between the outdoors and the interior of the house. Instead, the house has an airtight firebox with a stone veneer. The traditional masonry chimney was replaced by a chimney that is stud framed, stone veneered, and thermally separated from the main structure. The flue is made of insulating pumice stone. It is insulated with polyurethane foam around the roof penetration, and is sealed and taped to the airtight layer of the roof. The firebox has an external dedicated combustion air intake.

Framing members should never penetrate the structure of the insulated envelope, because that would create a thermal bridge. That is why the soffit and eave construction is structurally separated from the superinsulated envelope, and the roof joists never extend beyond the exterior sheathing. However, the Cleveland Farm house features one exception to this rule. There is a very large, structurally necessary, cantilevered overhang on the west side of the house, which shades the living room. To minimize heat loss through the thermal bridge, the overhang was insulated underneath with 2 inches of EPS and between the support beams with cellulose.

Making It Airtight

To make sure that the house was airtight, PHIUS suggested two lines of defense. These consisted of an exterior, continuous layer of house wrap, which was taped at all seams to avoid convection in the insulation layer, and an interior air barrier made up of carefully taped and plastered gypsum board. Areas where floor

To make their home energy independent, the family first built their house to meet the Passive House standard. Then, they installed a 5kW wind turbine (pictured on front cover), which they expect will generate more energy than they need.

plates or interior partition walls penetrated the interior airtight layer, creating a path for indoor air to mix with the outside air, received special attention to ensure the continuity of the airtight layer.

The structural engineer specified that the first-floor and second-floor joists should bear on the foundation and the exterior stud wall respectively, ending on the exterior rim joist, as is current framing practice. This made it a challenge to render the building airtight, because there are large avenues for air leakage where floor plates penetrate the exterior envelope. Air leakage around floor plate penetrations is very difficult to control. A preferable framing option is one in which the floor joist bears on the interior stud wall, and the exterior wall is balloon framed and continuously insulated. Since that wasn't the case here, a 3-foot strip of house wrap was placed around the edge of the floor along the entire perimeter of the floor plates. Beginning at the inside of the interior airtight layer—the gypsum board—the house wrap was laid over the top plate, around the rim joist, up and back under the sill plate, and inside again to connect with the gypsum board of that next-floor wall. The house wrap was taped and sealed to the top and sill plates of the interior wall framing and was eventually sandwiched between the drywall and the interior wall framing. In addition, all sill plates were gasketed, sealed, and caulked. The polyethylene vapor barrier under the slab in the basement was wrapped up around the edges of the slab, taped, and sealed to the sill plate of the basement wall.

Mechanical System

When designing the equipment needed to condition a high-performance building, standard construction practice is turned on its head. Ventilation requirements are considered first. Next comes dehumidification. Then cooling needs are assessed to determine if any

Project Data and Specifications of the Cleveland Farm

Location	West Tisbury, Massachusetts	**Wall framing**	Wall cavity 305 mm (12 in) double-wall framing; 2 x 4 interior, 2 x 6 exterior stud wall
Region and climate	*Latitude:* 41°22'48" *Longitude:* 70°40'12" *Elevation:* 89 ft Cold climate	**Wall insulation**	51 mm (2 in) polyurethane spray foam; 254 mm (10 in) dense-packed cellulose
Heating degree-days/ cooling degree-days	5,713/436	**Roof framing**	406 mm (12 in) TJIs
		Roof insulation	51 mm (2 in) spray foam polyurethane; 356 mm (14 in) blown-in cellulose
Year of construction	2007–2008	**Windows**	Wood/aluminum-clad frames with partial cork insulation; low-e, argon-filled, triple-pane glazing
Typology	Single-family residence		
Finished floor area	422 m² (4,544 ft²)		
Architect	Craig Buttner	**Ventilation system**	2 x 95% sensible efficiency ERV
Builder	Clancy Construction, LLC	**Heating/ cooling/ dehumidification system**	2 x 1,000W (3,400 Btu/h) electric-resistance defrost; 12,000 Btu mini-split for heating and cooling; 450 ft² electrical in-floor radiant heat in kitchen and bathrooms
Passive House Consultant	Passive House Institute US (PHIUS)		
Foundation	*Main house:* 254 mm (10 in) concrete foundation wall *Master wing:* slab-on-grade with frost wall	**DHW system**	10 m² (107.6 ft²) evacuated-tube solar thermal system with electric backup
Foundation perimeter insulation	51 mm (2 in) XPS		
Under-slab insulation	203 mm (8 in) EPS		

Active System requirement to become *plus energy/ carbon neutral*
5 kW wind turbine

further treatment is necessary, and finally heating is considered last.

The Cleveland Farm house has a volume of 50,888 cubic feet. Ventilating a building with this large a volume required the use of two ERVs, especially since both will be run at their lower, more energy-efficient speed setting. These ERVs are self-balancing—that is, they take in as much air as they exhaust—so they cannot underpressurize or overpressurize the house. The air circulates through 6-inch intake and exhaust ducts that are insulated and air sealed. To protect the ERVs from frost during the New England winter, two 1,000W

electric-resistance defrost units were integrated into the air intake within the heated envelope. These heaters are set to come on when the outdoor temperature drops below 23°F. This keeps the exchange medium of the ERVs from freezing. The ERV that was chosen is the only ERV on the American market whose motor is efficient enough to meet the PHPP requirement. PHIUS chose to use ERVs rather than HRVs because in winter an ERV recovers humidity from the outgoing air and keeps the air in the house from getting too dry. In summer it helps to lower the cooling load by filtering out outdoor moisture. Humidity sensors were installed in all the bathrooms to increase the ventilation rate when the air in the bathroom is too moist.

To dehumidify the house in summer and to provide some cooling, a small mini-split air-to-air heat pump, with a rated output of 12,000 Btu/hr, was installed in line with the ERVs. The airflow rate of the ERVs matches that of the heat pump. The mini-split has an airflow rate of 265 cubic feet per minute (CFM) at low speed. The ERVs together have an airflow rate of 223 CFM at low speed, and will match the low flow rate of the mini-split at medium speed. The mini-split can also provide up to 10 W/ft^2 of heat through the supply air that gets delivered to the living room and bedrooms. The heat pump has a coefficient of performance (COP) of 3.4.

The heat load in the Cleveland Farm house is approximately 1.3 W/ft^2. This is a higher heat load than is typical in central European climates. Only

0.9 W/ft^2 can be effectively transported through fresh-air ventilation. When the peak heat load exceeds 0.9 W/ft^2, additional point heat sources distributed throughout the space are necessary. To meet the heat load in this house, 450 square feet of electrical in-floor radiant heat was installed in the bathrooms and kitchen. The wood-burning fireplace, with its airtight firebox, is also used for heating. An evacuated-tube solar-thermal system with electric backup provides DHW.

The island typically experiences steady winds—sometimes very high winds—so the family chose to take advantage of this resource by installing a 5 kW wind turbine in the backyard. It is expected to produce on average 8,000 to 10,000 kWh of electricity per year.

Adapting Locally to Passive House Construction

Passive House principles and construction methods are unfamiliar and therefore pose a challenge for most builders and their crews. On Martha's Vineyard, the situation is slightly different. Due to a high-end construction market, the workforce is better skilled than most and is trained to pay attention to detail and quality. Framing techniques that emphasize airtightness and the elimination of thermal bridging are already practiced in standard new construction. Although the workforce is familiar with high-performance building methods, the airtightness that a Passive House requires is beyond even these best building practices. To update the skills of the contractor and his crew before construction got started, and to teach them how to build such a tight house, PHIUS held a one-day training session. The architect, the contractor, and even the family attended.

Almost all of the materials specified for this Passive House were ones that are commonly used in the United States, and the workforce needed no special training to use them. The only exceptions were the windows and doors, which were imported from Germany. The German windows were chosen because there are currently no wood-framed windows on the U.S. market that are equally airtight and have a comparable R-value, and the German doors were chosen for similar reasons.

Construction Cost

The construction cost for the Cleveland Farm house was $1.3 million, including all labor and materials. The learning curve for the contractor and construction crew added to the cost of labor. This cost would decline as the contractor and his crew gained more experience. The cost of the additional materials used for insulation and framing was offset by the significantly lower cost of the mechanical system, which cost only about a third as much as a conventional HVAC system.

Chapter 6

The Stanton House

A local Amish crew constructed the prefabricated wall panels and framing for the Stanton House.

For Margaret and Gregory Stanton, retirement meant moving from the suburbs of Washington, D.C., to Margaret Stanton's childhood home, in Urbana, Illinois. It also meant an opportunity to create a lifestyle that would minimize their impact on the environment and even give them a chance to grow their own food. They were also concerned about rising energy prices, especially now that they were going to be living on a fixed budget. So when they first heard about Passive Houses—so energy efficient and environmentally friendly—they knew that a house like that would be the ideal home for them. Not only would it let them live independent of volatile energy prices, but it would enable them to live a more sustainable lifestyle. The Stantons contacted e-co lab in the spring of 2007 to discuss renovating what would become their future home.

The Stantons' original plan was to retrofit and expand the home that Margaret had grown up in to meet the Passive House standard. The home, which had been built in the 1940s, was located 2 miles outside of Urbana. It had concrete block walls and a slab-on-grade foundation. Undertaking a retrofit that included accessing and superinsulating the existing foundation and the walls was going to be challenging. However, when Klingenberg examined the foundation and realized how deteriorated it was, it became clear that demolition and new construction would be the most economical approach.

The decision to demolish her family home, and let its physical presence go, was a difficult one for Margaret. But the home wasn't going to vanish entirely. It would be rebuilt on the same footprint, but expanded by an addition on the east side.

Ecological Design Principles

Margaret's late mother had been a firm believer in reusing, recycling, and being a good steward of natural resources, and she had passed these beliefs on to her daughter. Sustainability—minimizing a product's embodied energy and its overall impact on the environment—guided the selection of materials for the new house. Knowing that the old house was going to be demolished, the Stantons spent many days working diligently to harvest all the reusable materials from it. The Douglas fir from the old roof framing was in such great shape and so beautiful that it was used to make exposed architectural laminated beams, as well as railings and trim, which were eventually installed in various rooms in the new house. The full-height pine paneling was remilled, refinished, and used for wainscoting and paneling in the new family room. The hardwood flooring from the old house was refinished and used in the study and hallway on the new second floor.

The Stantons avoided using products that contained ozone-depleting agents such as XPS, or products that could increase global warming, such as the expansion agents in polyurethane spray foams. All interior finishes and paint were water based and VOC free. Otherwise, the Stantons avoided using fossil fuel products as much as possible. Floor finishes are finished concrete, tile, hardwood, and natural-fiber carpets. Instead of vinyl siding they chose fiber cement siding. The only fossil fuel–based foam product used for insulation was high- and low-density EPS—which is recyclable and the least harmful of the foams—under the slab. The roof is still asphalt shingle, chosen over a metal roof to stay within budget. The house was built with the idea that eventually it could be deconstructed and all of its components could be recycled—including the foam under the slab. It might be worth a lot in 40 years!

Design

The Stanton House is a prairie-style, three-bedroom, single-family residence, with 2,200 square feet of finished floor space, a generous wraparound porch, and an attached two-car garage. The main part of the house has two stories, but there is a single-story annex on the east side. This annex reduces the compactness of the house, thus reducing its thermal

PHIUS

Not only will a **Passive House** let them live **independent** of volatile energy prices, it will enable them to **have** a more **sustainable** lifestyle.

performance. To compensate for this disadvantage, more insulation was added to the walls.

The master suite and the family room are located in the annex, which features vaulted ceilings throughout. The family room is finished all the way to the ceiling with reclaimed pine paneling from the old house and has a wide picture window seat facing south. The master bedroom faces north and east, with scenic views overlooking nearby fields. It is separated from the family room by a closet, and a sliding door that is 4½ feet wide.

The living and dining rooms are on the first floor in the main part of the house, along with the kitchen and breakfast nook and a utility room, arranged much as they were arranged in the old house, and a powder room. The living room is separated from the family room by a wall that has a ventless fireplace on the living room side. The living room, which is continuous with the dining area, opens to the south lawn with two sets of three all-glass doors. A 2½-foot wraparound overhang in line with the first-floor roof fascia shades these glass doors in the summer; a similar overhang upstairs shades the upstairs windows.

On the second floor, a study above the dining area overlooks the two-story living room. A mechanical closet encloses the ventilation system. Two bedrooms, separated by a second bathroom, are located on the north side of the house.

The house is oriented toward true south to maximize passive-solar gain in winter. Glazing on the north, east, and west sides is minimized, to prevent thermal loss in winter and unwanted gain in summer. The overhangs and the roof of the wraparound porch provide the only external shading.

The location is the same as that of the Smith House, and therefore the climate is the same. Urbana has a winter design temperature of −3°F, with relatively high solar radiation. In order to create a superinsulated home in this climate, all six sides of the envelope must be insulated to at least R-56.

Construction Details

Wall Assembly

The wall assembly that forms the envelope of the house is actually a composite of two walls, so that the electrical and plumbing lines can pass through the interior wall without penetrating the exterior envelope. The exterior wall is a prefabricated panel. This panel is framed with 12-inch wooden I-joists set upright at 24 inches OC, and sheathed with structural fiberboard on the exterior

Moving from the balloon-framed panels of Fairview II, the single-story platform panels of the Stanton House prove easier to build and maneuver.

side and OSB on the interior. The structural fiberboard sheathing on the exterior has a higher perm rating than the OSB sheathing on the interior. The wall panel is designed to dry to the outside, so that any moisture that gets into the wall during the heating season can leave the wall through the exterior sheathing. A vented rain screen between this sheathing and the fiber cement

siding also helps to keep the wall dry. The interior OSB sheathing qualifies as a vapor barrier, as it has a perm rating of less than 1. It also forms the designated airtight layer on the inside. All joints in the OSB are carefully sealed and taped.

The interior wall is framed with standard 2 x 4 studs at 24 inches OC and drywalled. This interior wall protects the OSB sheathing on the inside of the exterior wall from accidental penetration by the occupants. Both walls are filled with a high-density fiberglass insulation, applied using the blow-in-blanket (BIB) system. Together, the two walls have an R-value of 64.

Roof
The roof structure consists of vented prefabricated roof trusses. They are filled with 20 to 24 inches of loose-fill cellulose, with a total R-value of 87. The Stantons chose asphalt shingle as the roofing material, since their budget did not allow for a metal roof.

Slab
The foundation consists of a continuously insulated thickened-edge concrete slab. The main area of the slab is 5 inches thick and rests on 12 inches of EPS. The thickened edge is 1½ feet wide and 18 inches deep, and it rests on 4 inches of high-density EPS. The thickened edge is surrounded by 2 inches of high-density EPS, which is covered with a slate finish around the base of the building. The slab has a total R-value of 51. The

interior side of the slab is exposed, finished with an acid stain, and sealed with a water-based sealer; it serves as the floor in the kitchen, living room, and dining room. The large thermal storage capacity of the concrete will help to modulate the indoor temperature year-round, but particularly in the summer in this climate.

Windows

All the windows are triple-pane argon filled, with a low-e coating and an SHGC of 0.52. The solid-wood frames with aluminum exterior cladding are insulated only where they meet the wall assembly. To mitigate the thermal bridging effect of the installation, 2 inches of XPS and 3 inches of cork were applied on the outside of the window frames, which were set 5 inches into the walls. These measures are sufficient to reduce heat loss in this climate; thermally broken frames, which would be needed in colder climates, are unnecessary here. All windows and doors have multipoint locks and are rated exceptionally airtight by the PHI.

Mechanical, Plumbing, and Electrical

Ventilation and Space Conditioning

The central component of the mechanical system is an ERV with a measured efficiency of 83% to 89% and a very energy-efficient fan motor. The ducts through the exterior wall that bring in fresh air and exhaust stale air

With practice, the Stanton House crew has become adept at building and assembling Passive House prefabricated panels and attending to details that will help ensure the home's performance.

are 7 inches in diameter, well insulated, and carefully sealed. Before entering the ERV, the incoming fresh air passes over a water-to-air heat exchanger integrated into the duct system. This heat exchanger preheats the air in winter and precools and dehumidifies it in summer. The "water" in the water-to-air heat exchanger is actually brine that is circulated by a 10W pump through a 300-foot-long closed ¾-inch PEX tubing loop, which is buried directly under the slab insulation. In winter the earth warms the brine to 45°F on average, and that warmth is transferred to the fresh air before it enters the ERV. Similarly, in summer, the below-grade soil cools the brine to about 60°F. A 1,000W electric-resistance element installed after the ERV further conditions the air when necessary.

The conditioned air is delivered through a small duct system consisting of 6-inch trunk and 4-inch branch lines. The air is dispersed through standard round adjustable diffusers, except in the living room and the family room, where European far-throwing diffusers are installed. Those diffusers push the air at a higher velocity into larger-than-normal rooms. This is achieved passively by the design of the diffuser (no additional fans are used to achieve a higher airflow rate). A 9,000 Btu mini-split air-to-air heat pump in the study provides additional point source heating and cooling. There are in-floor electric-resistance heaters in the bathrooms, and a gel-burning ventless fireplace in the living room that can deliver 9,000 Btu of heat.

PHIUS

To minimize the risk of radon entering the house, a continuous 6-inch layer of gravel was installed under the slab. As a second line of defense in case of cracks in the concrete, an 8-mil vapor and air barrier was installed on top of the gravel. The constant and generous supply of fresh air brought in through the ventilation system will dilute any radon gas that does enter the house to a harmless level.

Lighting and Appliances
To avoid penetrating the exterior envelope, all electrical installations, switches, and outlets are installed in the interior 2 x 4 wall. The main electrical supply, as well as the telephone and cable connections, enter the house through conduits from underneath the slab.

Recessed lighting was not installed in the exterior envelope, since it would have penetrated the airtight layer and reduced R-values significantly. Recessed lights were installed in the first-floor ceiling cavity and in the ceiling of the wraparound porch. CFL lighting and light-emitting diodes (LEDs) were used in all light fixtures. All appliances have the highest possible energy and water efficiency ratings. Since conventional clothes dryers and kitchen exhaust fans have exhaust ducts and

Project Data and Specifications of the Stanton House

Location	Urbana, Illinois
Region and climate	*Latitude:* 40°6'57" *Longitude:* 88°14'34" *Elevation:* 738 ft Cold climate
Heating degree-days/ cooling degree-days	6,359/888
Year of construction	2008
Typology	Single-family residence
Finished floor area	226 m² (2,430 ft², including 2-story space)
Owner	Margaret and Gregory Stanton
Builder	Darcy Bean Custom Construction Champaign, Illinois
Energy Consultant	Conservation Technologies Duluth, Minnesota
Foundation	Thickened-edge slab on 102 mm (4 in) high-density EPS
Foundation perimeter insulation	51 mm (2 in) high-density EPS
Under-slab insulation	305 mm (12 in) EPS
Wall framing	Exterior: vertical 305 mm (12 in) wooden I-Joists; interior: 2 x 4 stud wall
Wall insulation	305 mm (12 in) blown-in fiberglass; 89 mm (3.5 in) blown-in fiberglass

Roof framing	Prefabricated wood trusses with vent chutes under sheathing; interior: 2 x 4 stud
Roof insulation	508 mm (20 in) blown-in cellulose; 89 mm (3½ in) blown-in fiberglass
Windows	Wood/aluminum-clad frames with cork insulation; triple-pane, argon-filled, low-e glazing; overall U-value of glazing: 0.96 W/(m² K) (0.17 Btu/[h ft² F])
Ventilation system	95% sensible efficiency ERV
Heating/ cooling/ dehumidification system	1,000W (3,400 Btu/h) electric resistance element post heater; 9,000 Btu mini-split air-to-air heat pump; water-to-air heat exchanger; closed ground loop
DHW system	5.4 m² solar-thermal flat-plate collectors with 80 gal storage tank; electric backup

Active System requirement to become *net zero site energy*
2 kW PV system (not installed but wired in)

Active System requirement to become *net zero source energy*
4.5 kW PV system (not installed but wired in)

Active System requirement to become *plus energy/ carbon neutral*
5.2 kW PV system (not installed but wired in)

separate makeup air systems that require penetrations through the envelope, no such appliances were installed. Instead, the Stantons chose a condensing dryer and a recirculating kitchen exhaust system. The condensate from the dryer is drained into the existing plumbing system.

Water Services

The Stanton House is outside the city limits of Urbana, so it has no access to city water or sewer services. The Stantons get their water from a well; the supply pipe enters the house from underneath the slab. The house has a septic system. The Stantons also collect rainwater

This three-dimensional rendering of the Stanton House's living room shows off the double-story space and bank of south-facing windows.

PHIUS

in a cistern; they use it to irrigate the garden and yard, with a small PV-powered pump. A flat-plate solar-thermal collector system supplies hot water to a storage tank, and an electric water heater serves as a backup.

Plumbing and PV

The vent stack of the plumbing system is vented above the roof, as required by code in Illinois, and is insulated in its entirety on the inside of the building to meet the thermal requirements of a Passive House. The spigot that provides water from the house to the garden passes through a conduit sleeve that is filled with spray foam; the sleeve is taped and sealed to the interior airtight layer of the building. All pipe penetrations through the concrete floor are likewise sealed to make them airtight.

The Stantons are not planning to install a PV system right away, but the house is wired to accommodate a grid-tied PV system in the future.

Construction Cost

The Stanton House is an ambitious project—both in its energy efficiency and in its green features. Construction is expected to cost around $350,000. Assuming that the wraparound porch and the garage, with a combined total area of 1,151 square feet, cost an estimated $50,000, the cost per square foot will

be $97, based on the home's exterior dimensions. Using the finished floor area as the basis for this calculation, and including the second-story open space, brings the cost per square foot to $124. If the Stantons put in a PV system at the current cost per watt installed, and the home becomes plus energy/carbon neutral, the cost per square foot will be $146.

Without an active-solar system, the cost of the Stanton House residence is comparable to that of other custom homes in the area. But the end result will be substantially different: The Stanton House will require only 10% of the average energy used to heat and cool conventionally built homes in this climate. And its total energy consumption will be one-fifth that of a conventional home.

The cost to build this house is in line with those of other custom homes for several reasons. An experienced design team worked closely with the builder throughout the planning process to optimize all aspects of the home's construction. Very close attention was also paid to preconstruction communication among the trades and coordination during the construction process. Finally, the design team worked with the builder to assure the best quality control.

For more information:

To find out more about the **Stanton House**, visit **www.e-colab.org/ecolab/Projects.html**

Chapter 7

Toward a Passive House in a Hot-Humid Climate

From its white-tile roof and wide overhangs to its high-performance windows, this house's efficiency features make it a standout in Southern construction. Danny Parker, principal investigator on the design and construction of this energy-efficient house, is pictured at top right.

Conceived in northern Europe, the original Passive Houses were designed for heating climates. Adapting the design guidelines to a hot and humid climate would require both creativity and a good understanding of what makes houses work well in such an environment. Although no U.S. builder has stepped up to the challenge of constructing a certified Passive House in this type of climate, a home that meets many of the Passive House requirements has already been built.

In 1998, the Florida Solar Energy Center (FSEC) decided to test its ideas on how best to drastically reduce residential energy use in hot-humid climates by constructing a super-energy-efficient PV residence (PVRES) in Lakeland, Florida. Builder Rick Strawbridge and Lakeland Electric, the city of Lakeland's municipal utility, collaborated with FSEC on this project. The Lakeland PVRES uses just 37.6 kWh/m^2/yr—a total site energy consumption that is within the Passive House standard of no more than 44 kWh/m^2/yr site energy, or less than 120 kWh/m^2/yr total source energy.

To help FSEC test the effectiveness of various efficiency measures, Strawbridge constructed two side-by-side 225 m² (2,422 ft²) homes with identical floor plans and orientations. One home, the builder's standard model, met Florida's relatively stringent energy code. The other home included the most energy-efficient innovations and appliances the FSEC project team could find.

Why was FSEC so interested in designing a super-energy-efficient home? Because homes in hot-humid climates use far more electricity than the national average. Energy consumption for air-conditioning alone can run to 40 kWh per day during the summer months in Florida.

The team monitored the two homes for one year. During that year, the PVRES used 6,960 kWh of electricity and generated 5,180 kWh through the PV system. The home's net energy use for the year—the electricity that the utility provided—was just 1,780 kWh. For the same year, the standard home used 22,600 kWh, all of which the utility had to provide. Yearly energy savings for the PVRES were 70%, based on its total electricity use. Based on the electricity that the utility provided to each home—and taking into account the production of the PV system—yearly energy savings for the PVRES were an astounding 92%.

Perhaps even more important than these savings is the fact that during periods of peak electric demand, the PV system allows the PVRES to place nearly zero net demand on the grid. On average days, net power flows from the home to the grid almost continuously during daylight hours.

What Makes the PVRES So Efficient?

What accounts for this house's incredibly low energy use, even in one of the country's hottest climates? Most of its efficiency features would be no surprise to anyone familiar with the Passive House concept: It has high levels of insulation and high-performance windows. However, the FSEC researchers also brought decades of design experience to the table when figuring out how best to minimize the cooling load in a hot-humid climate. From overhangs to an improved air-conditioning system, the house's efficiency features make the PVRES a standout in Southern construction.

Wider Overhangs

Florida Cracker–style homes, built at the turn of the last century, before air-conditioning, had wide porches and deep overhangs. These were necessary to keep the house cool. However, with the advent of air-conditioning,

Based on the **electricity** that the utility provided to each home, yearly **energy savings** for the **PVRES** were an astounding **92%**.

On average days, net power flows from the home's PV system to the utility grid almost continuously during daylight hours.

many builders cut these overhangs short or sacrificed them entirely in order to save on construction costs. Rick Strawbridge's standard home has only 1½-foot overhangs.

The PVRES returns to tradition with 3-foot overhangs around the perimeter of the house. These overhangs cast a shadow nearly 6 feet long, shading most of the wall and at least 75% of the south and east window area. This reduces heat gain to the walls and through the windows, and also reduces glare inside the house.

Reflective Roofing

Over the last five years, FSEC has conducted numerous experiments showing that white roofs reduce cooling energy use. Tests in a dozen homes converted to white roofs showed an average cooling energy reduction of 19%. Indeed, FSEC tests on various roofing systems—radiant barriers, added ventilation, white-tile and white-metal roofs—showed that white tile gave the best cooling-related performance. In summertime, heat transfer through a white-tile roof was 76% lower than heat transfer through a black asphalt shingle roof. In keeping with this research, the PVRES features a white concrete tile roof, which was donated by the Monier Company. The roof of the standard home is conventional gray-brown asphalt shingle. The solar reflectance of the Monier white tile tested at 77%, while the solar reflectance of the asphalt shingle was only 7%. Both homes have R-30 fiberglass insulation blown into the floor of the unconditioned attic, which slows heat transmission from the attic to the conditioned space.

Exterior Wall Insulation

In conventional residential construction, masonry walls in Florida are insulated with R-3 to R-5 thin fiberglass batts or XPS, installed on the interior of the wall. Although R-3 to R-5 may seem quite low for those used to building practices in northern climates, field monitoring has shown that insulation installed on the interior of a wall can reduce the need for air-conditioning by only 5% to 10% in Florida's climate, if the walls are already a light color. Adding more insulation to the interior of the wall will further reduce the energy used for air-conditioning by only 1%, or so, because walls in a single-story home with good overhangs represent only a small part of the cooling load. However, insulation installed on the exterior of masonry walls can help reduce the need for air-conditioning during the late afternoon and early evening by increasing the time that a precooled building can stay comfortable without it. FSEC chose to pursue this strategy for the PVRES, particularly since precooling could be accomplished efficiently by running the air-conditioning in the late morning, when there is usually plenty of sunshine and PV output is approaching its maximum. By covering the outside of the concrete block walls of the PVRES with 1¼ inches of isocyanurate insulation, and increasing the R-value of the wall assembly by R-10, FSEC was able to reduce the size of the air-conditioning system and shift utility energy use to nonpeak hours. The insulation was donated by the Celotex Corporation, which worked with the builder to resolve any questions about the unusual exterior application.

Advanced Solar-Control Windows
Windows strongly affect the cooling load in Florida houses. Generally, windows need to have a low SHGC to keep out the sun's heat, and a low U-value to reduce the design cooling load. Most windows used in Florida homes do not meet these criteria. The typical Florida window is single-pane clear glass with an SHGC of 0.875, a U-value of 1.1, and an aluminum frame.

For the PVRES, a superior product was needed. However, a low SHGC was not the sole criterion. A window with a very low SHGC can have a dark tint that transmits very little visible light. This can reduce daylight to such an extent that occupants have to keep the lights on in the daytime. Physical appearance was also considered important, so dark-tinted glass and reflective glass (which has a low SHGC but gives the windows a mirrored look) were both ruled out. Instead, FSEC chose a spectrally selective glass—one that would transmit much of the light in the visible part of the solar spectrum, while blocking out IR and UV light, which cause the house to overheat and furniture to fade.

The choice was PPG Industries' Sungate 1000 solar-control windows, a low-e, double-pane, argon-filled product. These windows have an SHGC of only 0.38, but a daylight transmittance of 73%. The center-of-glass U-value is 0.24. To reduce heat transmission through the window frame, white nonconductive vinyl frames were specified, giving the window an overall U-value of 0.35. The windows are color neutral and provide excellent daylight transmittance.

Most visitors to the PVRES cannot tell by looking at them that these windows are any different from standard windows. However, the difference in transmitted heat is quite apparent. The improved glass reduced the required size of the air-conditioning system. With 384 square feet of glass in the floor plan, *Manual J* showed that standard windows would require a 4-ton cooling system, while the Sungate 1000 windows would have required only a 3.4-ton system—a difference of 0.6 tons, or 7,700 Btu per hour. In fact, the combined effect of the many heat reduction strategies made it possible to reduce the cooling system to only 2 tons.

Low-Friction Interior Duct System
An innovative design feature in the PVRES is its low-friction interior-mounted duct system. In conventional houses, including the standard home, the ducts are frequently undersized and are almost always located

in the hot attic. Research has shown that air handlers located in the attic can increase space cooling energy use by up to 30%. Tests at FSEC have shown that not only does the attic sometimes reach 135°F in Florida's summers, but heat transfer to the duct system can rob the air conditioner of up to one-third of its cooling capacity during the hottest hours. The reason is simple: R-6 flex ducts contain the coldest air in the home—about 60°F—and are exposed to the hottest temperatures.

To avoid this problem, and to help make it possible to downsize the air-conditioning system, FSEC designed the duct system so that it fits inside the conditioned space. Whatever heat is gained by the duct system is heat that is removed from the conditioned space. To hide the ducts, false dropped ceilings, lower cathedral sections, and chases were used throughout the interior. To avoid problems with leakage, the duct system was sealed with mastic and was tested.

Finally, the duct system was oversized, to minimize airflow resistance. This has two advantages. First, it provides critically important airflow across the evaporator. Second, it reduces the power of the air handler fan, making the system more efficient and less noisy. The air conditioner chosen was a 15 SEER single-speed system with a variable-speed indoor air handler.

Building the PVRES was a way to find out how to save as much energy as possible in a new Florida home, and how the efficiency measures would perform when combined with PV electric power.

Minimizing airflow resistance reduces the variable-speed fan's power draw, since the motor decreases its required power in response to lower resistance to airflow. With high airflow, low-friction duct systems have been shown to improve the efficiency of the cooling system by up to 12%, at essentially no cost. A Balometer—an instrument for measuring low volumetric flows—mounted on the return-air grille of the air handler was used to verify that the target airflow of 700 CFM per ton at full fan speed was achieved.

Tight House, Tighter Ducts

A Minneapolis blower door was used to measure the airtightness of the PVRES. The reading was 1,587 CFM_{50}, or 4.9 ACH_{50}, with an effective leakage area (ELA) of 69 square inches. This airtightness level does not meet the Passive House standard of at or below 0.6 ACH_{50}. Much of the leakage to the outside appeared to be from the 30 recessed-lighting cans in the ceiling.

A Duct Blaster was used to determine relative leakage in the return and supply sides of the duct system. Total CFM_{25} leakage from outside the conditioned space was 50 CFM_{25}, or about 0.021 CFM/ft^2—a low value. The PVRES, with its interior duct system, had as low a leakage to the outside as any house that FSEC has ever tested. The data suggest that for homes of this type, some system of mechanical ventilation, combined with an ERV, may be desirable to efficiently deliver a healthy IAQ.

PVRES Economics

Building the PVRES was a way to find out how to save as much energy as possible in a new Florida home, and how the efficiency measures would perform when combined with PV electric power. As such, the project was research oriented; it was not meant to be economically feasible. Nevertheless, FSEC tracked the cost of the various measures that were installed in order to assess their economic performance (see Table 6.1). The FSEC researchers used DOE-2.1E building energy simulation software (Energy Gauge USA) to estimate how much each measure contributed to cooling energy savings (see Table 6.2). When considering the impact of any one efficiency measure, it is important to keep in mind that many measures interact with one another. For instance, how much cooling energy do tight ducts save? That depends heavily on whether the ducts are located inside the conditioned space or outside it. And white roofs save considerably more cooling energy when the ducts are located in the attic.

Since this was a demonstration project, not all of the efficiency measures were cost-effective. However, several of them were reasonably cost-effective, including the interior duct system, the high-efficiency air conditioner, and the high-efficiency lighting and refrigeration. And some of the measures used in the project, although they were not cost-effective from an energy savings standpoint, had side benefits. For instance, a tile roof will last longer than a shingle roof, and this—together with the energy that it saves—makes a tile roof economically attractive. And the rooms in a house with high-performance insulated windows will be quieter and less prone to fluctuations in temperature than the rooms in a house with standard windows—a benefit that is difficult to measure in terms of simple payback, but a benefit nonetheless. Furthermore, there are ways to

Table 6.1. Cost of Efficiency Measures

Efficiency Measure	Cost
High-performance windows (materials)	$ 4,026*
High-performance windows (labor)	$ 240
White-tile roof (materials)	$ 5,528*
White-tile roof (labor)	$ 5,301
Wider overhang	$ 1,882
High-performance air-conditioning	$ 1,263
Interior duct system	$ 950
Exterior wall insulation	$11,500
Propane lines and gas appliances	$ 479
Solar water heater with propane backup	$ 2,989
High-efficiency lighting	$ 525*
Programmable thermostat	$ 225
Most efficient side-by-side refrigerator of size class	$ 298
Total	**$35,206**
Total less donations	**$25,127**

*Donated items

Table 6.2. Cooling Energy Savings

Efficiency Measure	Cost	Savings kWh ($)	Simple Payback (Years)
High-performance windows	$ 4,266	1,610 ($129)	33
White-tile roof	$10,829	1,342 ($107)	101
R-10 walls with exterior insulation	$11,500*	307 ($ 25)	460
Wider overhang	$ 1,882	537 ($ 43)	44
Interior duct system	$ 950	1,150 ($ 80)	12
High-performance air-conditioning	$ 1,263	2,376 ($190)	7
High-efficiency lighting	$ 525	1,479 ($118)	4
High-efficiency refrigerator	$ 298	388 ($ 31)	10
Solar water heater	$ 2,989	2,097 ($123)†	24
Utility-integrated PV system	$40,000	5,600 ($448)	89

* Cost of the wall system was very large because this was a first-time installation. In a mature market, cost would be half as much.

† Computed on the basis of 37.8 gallons per day raised from 75°F to 130°F; energy factor (EF) = 0.88 base tank. Annual backup propane consumption estimated at 32 gallons.

Table 6.3 Improvement Measures

Improves Performance	How
Specify more tile flooring in floor plan	Makes greater use of ground as a heat sink
Use sealed recessed cans for ceiling fixtures	Reduces air leakage
Install more of the PV array on west face	Improves peak period power (2 kW) production
Consider higher efficiency water-to-air heat pump	Improves cooling efficiency by 10%–20%

Reduces Costs	How
Use white-metal rather than white-tile roof	Reduces incremental cost of roofing and simplifies PV installation
Use R-5 insulation on interior of masonry walls	Greatly reduces cost of wall insulation
Use large-diameter flex duct for interior ducts	Simplifies sealing and reduces cost
Use integrated-storage solar water heater	Single-tank system reduces cost

reduce the cost of implementing some of the efficiency measures used in the PVRES. One way would be to use surround porches to keep solar radiation off the walls and windows, which could mean that less insulation would be needed on the walls. Other strategies are to use white-metal roofing, which is less expensive than white tile, and to use an integrated-storage water heater. These modifications would reduce the incremental cost of the various improvements by over $22,000 without affecting performance.

Improving the Efficiency of the PVRES

Based on the findings of this study, the following changes could be implemented to save even more energy in a home of this kind if that home were being built today (see Table 6.3). First, better appliances and HVAC equipment, such as an 18+ SEER heat pump, would enhance performance. Second, better air sealing would improve the airtightness of the home, combined with dedicated mechanical ventilation to achieve an adequate IAQ. Third, much could be done to reduce electronics loads. As heating-and-cooling loads are reduced, the energy used by electronics—even when they are turned off and just drawing power in standby mode—

represents a greater percentage of total energy use. Structured wiring could be installed to kick off standby loads. And an electrical metering device could provide instantaneous feedback to let occupants know how much electricity was being used at any given time.

Finally, more of the floor area should be tiled. Thermographic inspection of the two houses found that the tiled floor in both houses was acting as a heat sink. During the month of May, each square foot of tile was providing free passive cooling at the rate of about 3 Btu per hour at 77°F interior air temperature. This means that, if most of the 2,000 square feet of floor area were tiled, it would provide about half a ton of free cooling—6,000 Btu per hour—in early summer. In Florida, tiled floors have other advantages as well. They do not harbor dust mites, and they dry quickly in the event of a flood—a real concern in areas that are prone to hurricanes.

For more information:

To learn more about the **Lakeland House**, visit **www.fsec.ucf.edu/en/research/buildings/zero_energy/lakeland/index.htm.**

Chapter 8
A Passive House Retrofit

The house remains comfortable on even the hottest summer days, with a little bit of management. When the sun moves to the west side of the house, Nabih Tahan opens up a large umbrella on the deck to shade the west-facing windows.

When Nabih Tahan and his family decided to move back to Berkeley, California, from southeastern Austria, where they had been living for 13 years, they knew they would be moving back to an old house that needed work, starting with a new foundation. As long as he had to redo the foundation, it made sense to Tahan to upgrade all the other fundamentals—and create a building that would comfortably and efficiently house his family for years to come. Tahan had earned a degree in architecture from the University of California at Berkeley and became a licensed architect first in California and eventually in Ireland. His approach to designing and constructing homes had been greatly refined during his years building housing in Europe, where sustainability is a widely embraced design principle. Tahan naturally wanted to incorporate the latest European construction practices into the retrofit of his house. At the time that Tahan was starting to plan his remodel, the Berkeley City Council was debating the adoption of a green building initiative that would give permitting priority to buildings that were constructed using

environmentally sound practices. Tahan hoped that this local interest in supporting green building might mean that the permitting process for an energy-efficient remodel would go smoothly.

Getting the permits he needed did not turn out to be as straightforward as he had hoped it would but, with some flexibility on his part, he eventually succeeded. During the design stage of his project, Tahan contacted e-co lab to run some preliminary calculations to determine how he could best meet the Passive House standard in California. Tahan planned his project using these calculations as guidelines. As this book goes to press, he is the first person in the United States who has retrofitted a home with the goal of meeting the Passive House standard. At this time, his home meets the Passive House requirement for space heating, and he is continuing to work on his home to ensure that it will meet the other Passive House requirements.

In remodeling his house, Tahan had two main goals. The first was to construct a comfortable, energy-efficient home for his family. The second was to create an educational tool, to show visitors what a truly sustainable house looks and feels like. One of his long-term goals is to start a factory to manufacture prefabricated Passive House panels, in order to standardize this type of construction and make it

more affordable. He hopes his own home will generate sufficient interest in Passive Houses to make this possible.

Site Constraints

Tahan's house, which he bought in 1977, sits on a long, narrow lot—just 33 feet wide by almost 140 feet long. The zoning allows for two single-family dwellings as long as each house has an on-site parking space. From the standpoint of sustainability, it makes sense to plan for more than one house on such a centrally located site. There is easy access to rapid transit, and the site is within walking distance of offices, schools, shopping, and entertainment. Since the city planning department would not waive the parking requirement, Tahan had to figure out where to fit two parking spaces on the lot, to ensure that he could build a second house in the future. With no room in the front or on either side of the existing house, he had no choice but to try to squeeze one parking space almost inside the house itself. That constraint helped to define the look of his renovation. Tahan decided to jack up the existing structure, rebuild the too-short first floor so that the ceiling height now meets code, but its length is narrower by 7 feet than the second floor, and put one parking space alongside the new first floor; the second floor is cantilevered over the

Tahan's **approach** to **designing** and **constructing** homes had been greatly **refined** during his years building housing in **Europe**, where **sustainability** is a widely **embraced** design principle.

Nabih Tahan

rebuilt first floor. (A similarly creative solution will be needed for fitting in the second parking space when a second home gets built, should this parking requirement still be in force by then.) The first floor is now all-new construction; the second floor is totally retrofitted; and the two floors together form a 1,514 ft² home designed to meet the Passive House standard.

Rebuilding from the Ground Up

Tahan's use of highly energy-efficient construction techniques is apparent throughout, beginning with the foundation, which is insulated on all four sides. The 4-inch concrete slab rests on 1½ inches of XPS and is surrounded by another 1½ inches of XPS. The top of the slab is insulated with 3 inches of polyisocyanurate, which has a higher R-value per inch than XPS. In the mild climate that Tahan lives in, this above-slab insulation should obviate the need for any kind of in-floor heating system, whose costs would far exceed those of insulation and air sealing.

The new first floor consists of three bedrooms and one bath. The walls are framed with 2 x 6 studs set 24 inches OC and insulated with 5½ inches of blown-in cellulose for an R-value of 20. The exterior side is sheathed with ½-inch plywood, with a Tyvek Home Wrap waterproofing membrane installed over it. An air space and drainage plane was created on top of the Tyvek by installing a vertical layer of 1-inch by 2-inch battens at 1-foot intervals. In order to prevent insects from nesting in this air space, an insect screen was installed to fill the gap between the battens at the top and bottom of the wall. Half-inch cement board is installed on top of the battens, with a plaster coating as the final finish. The battens help to maintain the rigidity of the cement board by bridging the 2-foot gap between the studs.

The air space between the waterproofing membrane and the façade is a common detail in wood frame construction in Europe. Its purpose is to keep rain away from the structure and promote drying of the façade by increasing air movement around it. In Europe, it is called a drained and ventilated cavity, while in the United States it is called a rain screen. The façade acts as a jacket to the house, protecting it from the elements. Like a jacket, the façade needs to be durable and it must be able to dry quickly. In Tahan's home, the plastered cement board is the jacket on the first floor, while redwood siding is the jacket on the second floor.

The second floor was constructed in 1904. The existing walls dated from the original construction. They had been built with 2 x 4 studs set 16 inches OC. To improve the thermal resistance of these walls, Tahan had 3½ inches of cellulose blown in between the studs. He then installed ½-inch plywood sheathing, covered with Tyvek and flashed at the doors and windows, as he had done downstairs. A 2-inch layer of rigid foam insulation was installed on top of the Tyvek to achieve a total R-value of 26. Tahan installed battens on top of this insulation to create an air space, as he had done downstairs; he planned to then install wood cladding on top of the battens. First, though, he had to find an ultraviolet- (UV-) resistant, breathable waterproofing membrane with which to cover and protect the rigid insulation. He wanted this membrane to be dark, so that it wouldn't show through the gaps in the cladding, but he couldn't find a dark product, so he went with GreenGuard Housewrap, which is green. To give it additional UV protection and to prevent insects from nesting in the air space, he installed a full layer of insect screen over the battens. This had been unnecessary on the first floor because there were no gaps in the cement board.

The wood cladding on the second-floor is the reclaimed, old-growth redwood siding that had been protecting the building for 100 years. In order to reuse this siding, Tahan had it removed and planed to make it look new again. It was then installed with the old inner surface facing out. The top and bottom edges of the siding were cut at an angle so that any water that got in between the pieces would run down and drain off, rather than pool at these intersections and possibly cause rotting.

Cellulose insulation was blown in between all of the rooms in the house to keep the heat in each room, and to prevent the transmission of sound from room to room. Tahan also had cellulose blown in between the two floors. In many conventionally built homes, the floors remain uninsulated. Not insulating interior floors creates an uninsulated cavity around the perimeter of the floor through which significant amounts of heat can transfer from interior spaces to the outdoors. The second floor ceiling, which is the top of the building envelope, was also insulated to prevent heat transmission from the living spaces to the attic above. The attic is uninsulated and is used mainly for storage. It is reached through an insulated hatch made by Rainbow Attic Stair, an Austrian company. The door of the

hatch is insulated with 2 inches of Styrofoam, for an R-value of 15, and has two rows of gaskets to make it more airtight.

Since the climate in Berkeley is relatively mild, the windows are dual-pane, rather than triple-pane, with a U-factor of 0.35 and an SHGC of 0.32. Only two of the windows face south, just as they did in the original construction. The city planning department did not allow Tahan to add any new south-facing glazing, because that side of the house sits just 1 foot from the property line. The rest of the windows face east and west. There are 16-inch roof overhangs on all four sides of the house. This is another original construction feature that Tahan could not get permission to change. Although the overhangs are not as wide as Tahan would have liked them to be, the house remains comfortable in the summer, with a little bit of management. On the hottest summer days, he opens the windows early in the morning to cool the house. In the afternoon, when the sun moves to the west side of the house, he opens up a large umbrella on the deck to shade the west-facing windows. Even when the outdoor temperature rose above 95°F during his first summer in the house, the indoor temperature never exceeded 75°F.

Performance

To meet the Passive House standard for airtightness, Tahan had his team seal everything they could think of to seal. This included the doors and windows; all the blocking at the attic; the intersections between the wall framing and the glued, laminated, or glulam beams; and the holes around electric wires and plumbing pipes. They used expandable foam to seal the larger joints, and high-performance elastomeric sealant at the plywood joints and other small gaps. Then they ran a preliminary blower door test. It showed that the house was leaking 146 cubic feet (ft^3) per minute at 50 Pa—just over the 140 ft^3 per minute that the standard permits, given the volume of the house. They sealed up all the remaining leaks that they could find—specifically around the attic hatch and around the sheet metal pans under the doors. As of this writing, a final test had not been done.

The Passive House standard specifies mechanical ventilation—an absolute necessity anyway with such a tight house. Tahan installed an UltimateAir RecoupAerator 200DX ERV, which has an advertised efficiency of 95%. Supply ducts go to all the bedrooms and the living room, and exhaust ducts pull air from the bathrooms and kitchen. The bathrooms also have dehumidistats, which are programmed to kick the ventilator up to high when the bathrooms reach a certain humidity level. The ERV can also be controlled manually with a timer.

The second floor's outermost layer is the reclaimed, old-growth redwood siding that had been protecting the building for 100 years. Inside, the kitchen was remodeled and upgraded to give it a much more modern look.

To comply with California's Title 24 energy code, all of the bedrooms and bathrooms have electric baseboard heaters—one 1,000W heater and nine 500W heaters in all. The Title 24 calculations required a total heating load of 17,294 Btu, which is equivalent to 5,067 kW. While some supplemental heating will be

needed during the winter months, Tahan is looking into using a more efficient means of getting that heat than relying on the baseboard heaters. He is thinking of adding a hot water booster coil to the ventilation system, so that the supply air can be heated before it enters the bedrooms. The source for the hot water could be either solar panels or an instantaneous water heater. The Passive House standard limits heating energy use to less than 15 kWh/m^2a or 1.4 kWh/ft^2/yr, and Tahan thinks he can meet this requirement. In his case, it translates to about 2,100 kWh per year, or 5.8 kWh per day on average, for heating.

According to Tahan's utility bills, since he moved in seven months ago, his family has used an average of 12.3 kWh/day for all electricity use. During the summer months, when the baseboard heaters were not in use, Tahan averaged 8.4 kWh/day for lighting and appliances. Assuming that the use of lighting and appliances is constant throughout the year, Tahan estimates that they used an average of 3.9 kWh/day for heating only, over the few winter months in which he was in the house. Tahan made some preliminary calculations based on his family's energy use during his first seven months

in the house and estimates that he may be slightly exceeding the source energy requirement by year's end. He is considering several changes to lower his source consumption, including shifting his heating method from electric baseboard heaters to a hot water coil heated by natural gas or solar power.

Now that Tahan has lived in his remodeled house for eight months, he is more than ever convinced that all homes should be built to the Passive House standard. Not only does the technology exist to design and build truly sustainable homes, but these homes deliver excellent comfort and IAQ. Tahan says he has never lived in such a comfortable house in his life. Living there has also made him more aware of how much energy he uses each day. He recently bought a Kill-A-Watt, which measures the wattage being used by an appliance, so that he can better control how much electricity he uses for appliances, lighting, and heating. Knowing how and where energy is consumed is the first step, Tahan says, to living within a sustainable energy budget.

For more information:

To learn more about **Nabih Tahan's house**, visit **www.nabihtahanarchitect.com**

The clients wanted to build a home that would **last for generations** to come. They set **three environmental goals** for this project: **longevity**, **energy efficiency**, and **sustainability**.

Chapter 9
The Skyline House: A Passive House Challenge

The Skyline House presented a near-ideal opportunity to design a house with a low-energy envelope that would reduce energy use and associated CO_2 emissions by 75% to 80%, compared to a code-built house. Near-ideal for three reasons. First, the clients had a strong environmental focus and a comfortable budget. Second, the site offered good solar opportunities. And third, the clients' needs fitted readily into the naturally efficient form of a one-story house, with a lower-level floor that is set into the ground.

Goals

The clients were a young family with two children. They had a steeply sloped site in Duluth, Minnesota, with spectacular views of Lake Superior, and they wanted to build a home that would last for generations to come. They set three environmental goals for this project: longevity; energy efficiency; and sustainability.

As outlined below, the architect specified the measures that would best achieve these goals:

1. The house would accommodate the family's needs for decades to come.
   - single-floor living for adult occupants
   - durable construction.
2. The house would be highly energy efficient.
   - a superinsulated, airtight building envelope
   - passive-solar design
   - an integrated HVAC system that relies on renewable energy.
3. The house would be built with an eye to sustainability.
   - environmentally friendly materials
   - a flexible design that could readily adapt to the changing needs of family members as they age.

Obstacles

Like any good design challenge, the project was not without obstacles. For the environmental goals set forth above, the chief obstacles were climate, site constraints, and timing. The climate in Duluth is often cold, with 9,800 heating degree-days per year. Insolation is fairly good at the site, but it is sometimes compromised by Lake Superior's cloud effect. Other site constraints included the steep slope and a narrow lot. In addition, the best views were found at 30° to 45° east of south, which meant that the orientation best adapted to take advantage of these views was not ideal for passive solar. Finally, since this was not originally intended to be a Passive House project, PHPP analysis and modeling were begun only after construction drawings were under way, when it was too late to make any major changes.

Energy Modeling

The 2,660 ft^2 house, which has three bedrooms, two bathrooms, and an attached two-car garage, was first modeled with REM:Design. When the calculation showed an estimated peak heating load of 8 Btu/ft^2 (a number that roughly correlates to a 65% to 70% reduction in energy use compared to a code-built house of the same design), the clients became excited about the prospect of improving the design to a level that might achieve Passive House certification. The house was then modeled using the PHPP software package.

The detailed and extensive modeling approach led to some changes in envelope design. Already-aggressive insulation levels were increased in the walls and ceiling and under the slab. The goal for airtightness was increased, and geothermal tempering loops were added to the design to preheat the incoming air for the mechanical ventilation system.

Since the attempt to meet the Passive House standard began well into the design process, some changes (in particular to site orientation) that might have made meeting the standard easier were deemed unfeasible. In addition, the recently translated software package contained some confusing language that may have led to some mistakes in data entry. Nonetheless, the software proved a valuable tool; it helped the architect to decide how best to design an ultralow-energy house in a very cold climate. The PHPP calculated energy for heating on the Skyline House is 23 kWh/m^{2}a, or 7.3 kBtu/ft^2/yr. The final calculated heating loads for the Skyline House, using both REM and PHPP, correspond to a reduction in energy use of about 75%, compared to use for a house of the same size in the same location built to Minnesota code.

The design relies on a very-high-performance envelope and passive-solar heating to lower annual loads. The two floors are stacked to achieve the optimal surface area-to-volume ratio for the building. Heat and

The Skyline House sits high atop Lake Superior's north shore.

DHW are delivered with a whole-house combination system using solar-thermal storage with a gas-fired backup. A geothermal ventilation air-tempering system optimizes the use of renewable energy. Finally, an airtight wood stove with direct-combustion air supply provides another means of using a renewable fuel source to help heat the home.

Although the home's modeled specific heating energy requirement is exceptional for the challenging climate of Duluth, it narrowly misses meeting the Passive House standard for heating demand. However, the house did end up meeting the primary-energy requirement of the standard. In spite of not meeting all of the requirements of the Passive House standard, the Skyline House embodies Passive House principles and uses Passive House building components in an exemplary way.

HVAC and Plumbing

A 48-tube (120 ft²) evacuated solar-thermal array is combined with a backup gas-fired on-demand water heater to provide space heating and DHW. Bathrooms and plumbing runs are clustered, and are located close to the mechanical room to reduce distribution heat loss.

The solar-thermal array heats water that is delivered first to an 80-gallon DHW storage tank. When that tank reaches a set temperature, the solar-thermal energy is diverted to a 275-gallon thermal storage tank. The larger tank acts as additional energy storage that can be transferred to the DHW tank or used for space heating. The output from the DHW storage tank runs through the on-demand water heater, which acts as a boost when the system needs a rise in temperature. One distribution loop from the thermal storage tank provides hydronic floor heat on the lower level and to the bathroom on the

The Skyline House provides beauty and comfort in a very cold climate.

system. Fresh air is delivered to all living spaces and exhausted from the bathrooms and kitchen. An independent makeup air system was installed to balance the kitchen range exhaust.

Two geothermal loops of PEX tubing, filled with a mixture of water and propylene glycol, one deep under the house slab and one underground outside the house, connect to a water-to-air heat exchanger in the outdoor air duct of the HRV to temper the ventilation air. This system prewarms the ventilation air in winter and precools it in summer. Passive-solar design and good cross-ventilation reduce the need for air-conditioning.

upper level. A second loop distributes warm air to the upper level via the ventilation system.

Ventilation Strategies

The Passive House standard requires mechanical ventilation with heat recovery. This is considered best practice in any case where the house is very tight and minimum use of energy is desired. The Skyline House has a whole-house, balanced, highly efficient HRV

Careful Construction

Most of the construction methods and materials required only minor alterations to standard practice. Extra attention was paid during construction to airtightness and to maintaining the integrity of the defined thermal boundary. The contractor and the building performance specialist stayed in close communication, and most potential problem areas were identified before detailed work was done in those

Project Data and Specifications of the Skyline House

Location	Duluth, Minnesota
Region and climate	*Latitude:* 46°46'58" *Longitude:* 92°6'21" *Elevation:* 1,424 ft
Heating degree-days/ cooling degree-days	9,818 /180
Year of construction	2007
Typology	Single-family residence
Finished floor area	247 m² (2,660 ft²)
Owner	The Leitz-Narjan Family
Architect	Wagner Zaun Architecture
Builder	J & R Sundberg Construction
Energy/Building Performance Consultant	Conservation Technologies
Foundation	8 in poured concrete walls insulated with 5 in EPS integral to the ICF and 4 in XPS added to the exterior of the ICF
Under-slab insulation	12 in XPS
Wall framing	2 x 4 double-stud wall 16 in OC
Wall insulation	14 in dense-packed cellulose
Roof framing	26 in parallel chord trusses with continuous vent chutes
Roof insulation	24½ in blown-in cellulose
Windows	Insulated fiberglass frames; triple-pane low-e glazing with superspacers, argon-filled *South windows:* SHGC 0.5, U-value 0.19; *North, east, west windows:* SHGC 0.3, U-value 0.17
Ventilation system	85% efficient HRV
Heating/ cooling/ dehumidification system	Solar-thermal hydronic heating system, with in-floor radiant tubing; water-to-air heat exchanger integrated in duct work after ventilation system; water-to-air heat exchanger closed ground loop integrated in duct work before ventilation system; pellet stove
DHW system	10.6 m² (114 ft²) solar-thermal vacuum tube collectors with gas-fired backup

Active System requirement to become *net zero site energy*
3 kW PV system (not installed but wired in)

Active System requirement to become *net zero source energy*
4.5 kW PV system (not installed but wired in)

Active System requirement to become *plus energy/carbon neutral*
5.6 kW PV system (not installed but wired in)

Rachel Wagner

Low-angled sun warms the interior in winter.

areas. A smooth and successful construction process was made possible by ongoing communication between the trades and the design and performance consultants. The general contractor knew why envelope performance goals had been set so high, and he understood the clients' priorities. The designer and building performance specialist set the tone and the expected level of performance for all of the subcontractors, and the general contractor helped coordinate a process designed to facilitate excellence. The home's airtightness, which was tested with a blower door and measured 0.7 ACH$_{50}$, is superb even though it narrowly exceeded the Passive House requirement of 0.6 ACH$_{50}$.

Construction was completed at the end of 2007. Actual energy data were not available as this book went to press.

Product Directory

DIAGNOSTIC TOOLS TO MEASURE BUILDING PERFORMANCE

The Energy Conservatory (TEC) is known worldwide as a leader in the building performance testing industry. Since 1981, our goal has been to provide building professionals with the specialized tools and support needed to create more efficient, affordable and healthy buildings. TEC continues to set the standard for specialized airflow and pressure measuring devices used to monitor and analyze the complex interactions which determine building performance.

Innovative design and careful engineering have given

TEC a reputation for providing the most reliable, accurate and versatile performance testing products on the market today. The Energy Conservatory has an experienced staff of professionals with a wide range of technical skills and field experience. When your personnel have questions on the use of our products or how to handle unusual situations they encounter, you can count on us to give dependable answers.

For more information visit our website at www.energyconservatory.com. Or give us a call at 612-827-1117.

Resources

Arthur Morgan Institute for Community Solutions
Yellow Springs, OH
Pat Murphy, Executive Director
(937) 767-2161
info@communitysolution.org
www.communitysolution.org
Community Design Consultants

Brach Design
Salt Lake City, UT
Dave Brach AIA
(801) 865-7648
contact@brach-design.com
www.brachdesign.com
Architect & Passive House Consultant

BriggsKnowles Architecture
Providence and New York
Laura Briggs
(212) 844-9060
briggsl@newschool.edu
www.briggsknowles.com and
www.do_it_together.org
Architects & Passive House Consultant

Building Energy Solutions, Inc
Placitas, NM
Larry Gorman, President
(505) 269-2969
lgorman3@comcast.net
www.buildingenergysolutions.com
Energy Modeling and Consulting

Byggmeister, Inc
Newton, MA
Paul Eldrenkamp, President
(617) 527-7871
paul@byggmeister.com
www.byggmeister.com
Design-Build & Passive House Consultant

Chris Benedict, R.A.
New York, NY
Chris Benedict R.A., Principal
(212) 477-6016
cbenedict@chrisbenedictra.com
chrisbenedictra.com
High Performance Design, Construction and Passive House Consultant

Coldham & Hartman Architects
Amherst, MA
Bruce Coldham
Thomas RC Hartman, Principals
(413) 549-3616
Bruce@ColdhamAndHartman.com
Tom@ColdhamAndHartman.com
www.ColdhamAndHartman.com
High Performance Building Design

Conservation Technologies
Duluth, MN
Mike LeBeau, Owner
(218) 722-9003
info@conservtech.com
Energy and Passive House Consultant

Darcy Bean Custom Construction
Champaign, IL
Darcy Bean Sr., Owner
(217) 398-4919
darcy@darcybean.com
www.darcybean.com
"We are moving in the right direction"

ecohousesantafe
Santa Fe, NM
Klaus Meyer, Owner
505-699-7080
klaus@ecohouse-santafe.com
ecohousesantafe.com
High Performance Construction

Energy Independence Corps
Fairfax, VA
John R. Essig, Director
(703) 980-1189
www.eicorps.com
Engineering, Design & Consulting for
Energy Independence

Energysmiths
Meriden, NH
Marc Rosenbaum PE
603-469-3355
marc@energysmiths.com
www.energysmiths.com
Design, Consulting, Training

Enviro Comfort Inc
Rockford, MI
(616) 433-9353
envirocomfort@ymail.com
www.envirocomfort.biz
High Performance Insulation Contractor
Utilizing Recycled and Renewable
Materials.

Equilibrium Energy Spaces
South Central Michigan
Christina Snyder
Registered Architect & Builder
(734) 428-9249
CASnyder@ic.org
public.casnyder.fastmail.fm
Passive House Consultant & Designer

Ferut Architects
Elyria, OH
Joseph Ferut, Jr., Architect
(440) 323-9930
joe@ferutarch.com
www.ferutarch.com
Sustainable Design in High Performance
homes

Green Built™ Michigan
Lansing, MI
(517) 646-2560
www.greenbuiltmichigan.org
Non-profit Promoting and Certifying
Green Built™ MI Homes

HarvestBuild Associates
Cleveland, OH
Mark Hoberecht
(440) 236-3344
www.harvestbuild.com
Innovative Strawbale PH Solutions,
Design, Consulting, DIY Training

Hayden Robinson Architect
Seattle, WA
Hayden Robinson AIA, Principal
(206) 691-3445
email@haydenrobinson.com
www.haydenrobinson.com
Passive House Consultant and Design

Hurst Construction
Sonora, CA
Chris Hurst, Master Builder
(209) 743-2638
www.zeropowerhouse.com
Design, Drafting and Construction
Since 1986

ICMC, INC.
Martha's Vineyard, MA
Gino Mazzaferro, Principal
(508) 696-8500
www.icmc-inc.com
High Performance Design & Construction

Jesper Kruse Construction
Greenwood, ME
Jesper Kruse, Owner
207-665-2371
mainepassivehouse@live.com
www.mainepassivehouse.com
High Performance Builder

McIntyre Builders, Inc
Rockford, MI
Arn McIntyre MSEng
(616) 696-1890
info@mcintyrehomes.com
www.mcintyrehomes.com
National Energy Value Housing Award recipient

Newell Instruments, Inc.
Urbana, IL
Ben Newell, President
(217) 344-4526
info@newellinstruments.com
www.newellinstruments.com
Passive House Mechanical Systems

One Earth Design
Taos, NM
Joaquin Karcher Dipl Ing
(575) 758-9741
oneearth@taosnet.com
www.oneearthdesign.com
High Performance Residence Design

Quantum Builders
1454 B 4th Street
Berkeley, CA
(510) 559-3488
info@quantumbuilder.com
www.quantumbuilder.com
Progressive Building Technologies

Remodel Guidance
Fairfax, CA
Graham Irwin, Principal
(415) 258-4501
info@remodel-guidance.com
www.remodelguidance.com
Passive House Consultant

Southface, LLC
McCall, ID
Jim Olson
(208) 630-3530
jimmy@southfaceconstruction.com
Cold Climate, Passive House Consultant

Sunpower Homes, Inc.
Denver, CO
Lance Wright, President
(303) 875-3228
greenenergyman@yahoo.com
www.passivehousecolorado.com
Passive House Consultant & Construction

Tad Everhart
Portland, OR
(503) 239-8961
mteverhart@comcast.net
Passive House Consultant

TE Studio
Minneapolis, MN
Tim Eian, Assoc. AIA
(612) 246-4670
tim@timeian.com, www.timeian.com
Passive House Consultant and Design

Tiptoe Energy
Ithaca, NY and Davis, CA
Mary Graham
mary@tiptoeenergy.com
Passive House Consultant

Transsolar Inc
New York, NY
David White
(212) 219-2255
www.transsolar.com
newyork@-trans-solar.com
Energy Efficiency Consultants, Passive House Consultant

UltimateAir, Inc.
Athens, OH
Jason Morosko, VP Engineering
(800) 535-3448
jmorosko@ultimateair.com
www.ultimateair.com
Balanced Ventilation Systems

Wagner Zaun Architecture
Duluth, MN
Rachel Wagner, Partner
(218) 733-0690
rwagner@wagnerzaun.com
www.wagnerzaun.com
Architecture and High Performance Home Design

About the Authors

Katrin Klingenberg is executive director and lead designer at **e-co lab**, a nonprofit community housing development organization. She and Passive House builder Mike Kernagis cofounded the **Passive House Institute United States (PHIUS)** to disseminate information about, and promote the construction of, Passive Houses in this country. She has designed and built several Passive Houses in the U.S. and consulted on numerous other Passive House projects throughout the U.S. and Canada. Recently Klingenberg worked with Dr. Wolfgang Feist, founder of the Passivhaus Institute in Darmstadt, Germany, to translate the energy-modeling software program, *Passive House Planning Package (PHPP)*, into the English language. Klingenberg has taught building science and design studios at the University of Illinois in Chicago and at Urbana-Champaign and has presented on the Passive House topic at national conferences and abroad. She is a licensed architect in Germany, and she received a master's degree in architecture from Ball State University in Indiana.

Mike Kernagis is construction manager and builder at **e-co lab**, as well as cofounder and administrator of the **Passive House Institute United States (PHIUS)**. Kernagis oversees the construction process of e-co lab's Passive Houses and delivers feedback from the site to the drawing table. Additionally, he provides Passive House best-practice training to home builders on the job site and supports educational initiatives through the development of seminars, trainings, tours, and the annual **North American Passive House Conference**. Kernagis has been in construction since 1990. He received his bachelor's degree in political science from the University of Illinois in Urbana-Champaign.

Mary James is the editor and publisher at **Low Carbon Productions** and was previously the editor and publisher of *Home Energy* magazine for ten years. She completed a science journalism graduate program at the University of California, Santa Cruz. She also received a master's degree in environmental policy analysis from the University of California at Davis.